JIHAD!

Understanding the
THREAT
of the
ISLAMIC STATE
to
AMERICA

By Ilana Freedman

This book may be reproduced, distributed and
transmitted for personal and non-commercial use.
Contact the Center for Security Policy
for bulk order information.

For more information about this book, visit
SECUREFREEDOM.ORG

Real Risk Management is published in the United States
by the Center for Security Policy Press,
a division of the Center for Security Policy.

ISBN-13: 978-1535274234
ISBN-10: 1535274239

Book Design by Jim Watson
Cover Design by J.P. Zarruk

The Center for Security Policy
1901 Pennsylvania Avenue, NW, Suite 201
Washington, DC 20006
Phone: 202-835-9077
Email: info@SecureFreedom.org
For more information, visit SecureFreedom.org

CONTENTS

FOREWORD

The phenomenon that is the Islamic State (IS) seemed to burst onto the world scene with lightning military advances across the former states of Iraq and Syria during the summer of 2014. Led by an Iraqi scholar of Islamic jurisprudence who goes by the *nom de guerre* Abu Bakr al-Baghdadi and who was named by a senior *Shura* council "Caliph Ibrahim," IS re-established the Islamic Caliphate for the first time in nearly 100 years. In so doing, it fulfilled the hopes and dreams of hundreds of millions of Muslims the world over who had been devastated by the 1924 abolition of the last Ottoman Caliphate by Kemal Ataturk in the wake of World War I. Indeed, one of the two clearly stated objectives of every jihadist group, from the Muslim Brotherhood to al-Qa'eda, has been precisely the re-establishment of the Caliphate (the other being imposition of Islamic Law, or sharia, worldwide).

The savage brutality of IS commanders in their strict enforcement of sharia in the cities and towns they overran shocked the world, which had not seen such levels of jihadist barbarity since the Ottoman genocide against Armenian Christians and others a century before. Few understood the self-defined role of Abu Bakr al-Baghdadi and the Islamic State as the vanguard of an Islamic Reform Movement, very much in the pattern of the first Caliph, Abū Bakr 'Abdallāh bin Abī Quḥāfah aṣ-Ṣiddīq, who led the *Ridda Wars* after the reported death of Muhammad in 632 to force relapsing tribes back under the black flag of Islam, much as IS does today.

To help illuminate the reality of the Islamic State, author Ilana Freedman delves into its core Islamic identity and the grave threat it poses to the United States and others in the Free World in this first monograph of a new Center for Security Policy series, The Terror Jihad Reader Series, a companion to its Civilization Jihad Reader Series. *Jihad! Understanding the Threat of the Islamic State to America* defines this enemy accurately, clearly explaining its motivations, intentions and abilities – without hyperbole and, instead, with careful scholarship. Ms. Freedman makes plain that, sadly, this monograph is but an snapshot of an organization about which additional chapters of Islamic jihad are yet to be written.

Among the most important contributions that Freedman brings to this topic is the frank treatment of the doctrinal sources that IS uses to justify its stupefying cruelty: The Quran, *hadiths, Sirat* and, of course, sharia. She makes clear that the brutality of the *hudud* punishments, sex-slavery, and cultural and ethnic destruction are not mere wanton psychopathy, but firmly grounded in established Islam as authenticated by the senior jurists and scholars, and accepted by the many millions of the world's Muslims.

Also especially revealing is Ms. Freedman's meticulous documentation of the Islamic State's organization, senior leadership and funding sources. She explains why it is that, even as the Islamic State loses territory previously conquered, it continues to expand – at least in the sense of securing the allegiance of individual Muslims and groups from across the world, including some which previously had been counted among the ranks of other jihadist organizations.

The lesson – and the warning – for the United States, the West and the remaining Free World in general is that the "Islamic State" is but a brand name, a flavor-of-the-week even. It had its predecessors and, if actually defeated, will spawn successors, as well.

Islamic supremacism and its driving ideology of sharia and the jihad it commands will endure until thrown on the ash heap of history, not just crushed on the battlefield and in cyberspace, but shown to be a losing proposition to Muslims and an abomination to others who insist upon living free rather than being subjugated beneath the yoke of Islamic tyranny.

At a time when the focus of the Islamic State increasingly is turning toward the *Dar al-Harb* (House of War), the Center for Security Policy offers *Jihad! Understanding the Threat of the Islamic State to America* in the hope that it will help inform and arouse freedom-loving peoples with regard to the threat that IS and the global movement of which it is now the vanguard pose to our most cherished freedoms and guiding principles – and why they must be defeated.

Frank J. Gaffney, Jr.
President
Center for Security Policy
July 2016

INTRODUCTION

F or thousands of years, the Middle East has been a cauldron of political, social, and religious unrest. Countless armies have marched across the barren deserts, clashing with each other for supremacy, and spilling the blood of innocents from time immemorial.

In 2011, the phenomenon called the "Arab Spring" initiated a new round of war and chaos that has now engulfed the Middle East, North Africa, and beyond. In December 2010, Tarek al-Tayeb Mohamed Bouazizi, a 26-year-old Tunisian street vendor, set himself on fire to protest government harassment and the confiscation of his scales. His death triggered a local uprising, which was inflamed by youths with "a rock in one hand, a cell phone in the other."[1]

The event triggered demonstrations, which were quickly pre-empted by the Muslim Brotherhood. Riots rapidly metastasized far beyond the region, spreading first to Egypt, Bahrain, Yemen, Libya, and Syria, then helped give rise to a revived al-Qa'eda in Iraq (AQI) and its successors, before finally reaching directly into the heart of Europe and the heartland of America.

The complexities that characterize the evolving cast of players, the growing number of groups aligning themselves with violent jihad, the shifting relationships among the various jihadi groups, combined with the reluctance of the Western nations to take a firm position in the growing conflict, have all combined to create conditions that seem to defy resolution or containment.

Out of the smoke of this deadly conflict first arose The Islamic State in Iraq and al-Sham, which then became simply the Islamic State (IS), or The Caliphate—the wealthiest and arguably the most powerful jihadist organization since the Ottoman Empire. The rise of the Islamic State has presented the world with a challenge not seen since the early 20th century but very much the norm during the hundreds of years following the 7th century establishment of Islam.

---

[1] According to Rochdi Horchani, a relative of Bouazizi and a witness to his self-immolation. "Between a Rock and a Cell Phone: Communication and Information Technology Use during the 2011 Egyptian Uprising" http://www.iscramlive.org/ISCRAM2012/proceedings/185.pdf

IS is the pure embodiment of Islamic doctrine, law, and scripture as exemplified by the life of Muhammad. It does not abide by any Geneva Conventions. It conquers and acquires territories, terrorizes the populations it conquers, steals the wealth from their farms and factories, sells the non-Muslims it conquers into slavery or murders them on the spot, destroys churches and ancient landmarks in order to erase any symbols of non-Islamic society, strips the regions it controls of its wealth, and leaves the people who remain without hope.

For IS, there is no compromise. Its mission is the mission of Islam: to conquer the world for Allah as commanded in the Qur'an.

In the third issue of its glossy magazine *Dabiq*, IS makes its point very clear. On the cover is a rendering of Noah's ark, floating on a raging sea. Underneath the picture is a caption: "It's either the Islamic State or the flood." For the Islamic State, the path of Islam is the only way, and that part of humanity that does not accept it will be lost in the deluge.

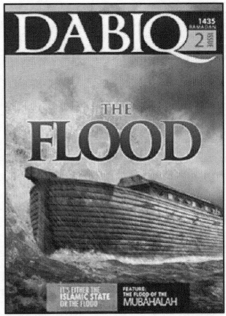

In the face of such a rising tide, the United States and its Western allies have been largely bereft of a policy that could effectively counteract the growing threat and accelerating chaos. The vacuum created by Western indecision, or worse, indifference, opened the door wide to a flood of Islamic terrorism.

IS grew out of an al-Qa'eda franchise in Iraq (AQI), and became a menace that rivals in savagery and barbarity anything the world has seen since the unspeakable horrors of the Nazi Holocaust. In the absence of effective leadership to stop it, IS grew increasingly powerful, and while the world yawned and went back to sleep, the growing slaughter of innocents turned into genocide.

What makes IS unique is its effective combination of irregular warfare and quasi-statehood under of the strict enforcement of shariah.

IS fights to purify Islam much as the Wahhabis have done since the seventeenth century. It fights against other Muslims for not adhering to the doctrine, laws, and scripture of Islam as commanded by Allah through Muhammad, the founder of Islam. In this, IS intentionally models itself on the example of Abu Bakr, the first Caliph after Muhammad, who fought the Ridda Wars to force backsliders to return under the banner of Islam.

Between June 2014, when IS declared its caliphate, and November 2015, the terrorist organization is known to have murdered more than 3,400 men, women, and children in Syria alone. At least 3,000 of them were unarmed civilians,[2] murdered with the most brutal savagery imaginable. Because there is insufficient documentation available, and because many of those in Syria whose murders were attributed to Syria's President Bashar al-Assad were actually the victims of IS, those estimates may, in fact, be extremely low.[3]

The rolling revolutions that spread from country to country in the course of the "Arab Spring" all had a common theme: the fall of largely secular, pro-Western autocracies and the dramatic shift to anti-West, Islamic-dominated governments. What followed hard on the heels of the "Arab Spring" in almost every country in which it occurred was chaos. Uprisings, planned, launched, orchestrated by al-Qa'eda, Muslim Brotherhood & other forces of jihad, and naïvely joined by students and young idealists seeking a more democratic society and freedom from tyranny, devolved into bloody, chaotic wars, spanning the region from West Africa to Southeast Asia. New Islamic governments were installed that ruled under the iron fist of shariah. And to further inflame the chaos, countless groups of jihadis ran rampant throughout many of these countries, jockeying for position, terrorizing the civilian populations, and fighting with each other as much as against the influence of their common enemy, the West.

Rather than standing fast with imperfect allies, who nevertheless had helped hold the line against the forces of Islamic terror, the United States, under the presidency of Barack Obama, consistently supported Islamic groups like the Muslim Brotherhood in Egypt, the Muslim Brotherhood and al-Qa'eda militias in Libya, and scores of fractured "rebel" groups in Syria, most of which were jihadist in ideology, including al-Qa'eda proxies like Jabhat al-

[2] According to the British-based Syrian Observatory for Human Rights. http://www.syriahr.com/
[3] "Was Al-Assad Responsible for the Sarin Gas Attacks in 2013? Or Was It ISIS?" by Ilana Freedman and Jerry Gordon. October 20, 2014. http://freedmanreport.com/?p=1959

Nusra and others. This ill-advised but unfailing support for jihadis in every case contributed heavily to the huge number of civilian deaths at the hands of terrorists and governments alike. The deteriorating fabric of life in Libya, Syria, and Iraq created a vacuum that was ripe for takeover by IS, which quickly became the most powerful of all the terrorist groups that roamed the region and now threaten the world.

The Islamic State is unflinching in its efforts to employ and exploit the most brutal practices of Islamic Law, some not seen since the Armenian genocide of the early 20th century. In in so doing, it has created an alarming new threat to the West. In just a few years, since its rapid rise to power, IS supporters, cells, and satellite groups have appeared with alarming speed in locations throughout the Middle East, Africa, Europe, and North and South America. Many of these represent either pre-existing Islamic terror groups that transferred allegiance to IS, or Muslims from among populations already deeply embedded in Western & other societies. Wherever it has appeared, IS has left a trail of horror including theft on a massive scale, the rape of thousands of women and children, crucifixions, beheadings, torture, dismemberment, and mass murders - all in ostentatious obedience to the commandments of Islam.

The Islamic State is a work in progress and has not yet reached a plateau in its development. It is still evolving at a rapid pace through the stages of its growth to maturity: the formation of its core fighting force, the conquest of territory from which to establish its caliphate, the development of its administration, and its proliferation into the West. That IS has achieved so much in so little time is testimony to its combination of unfettered determination, strategic brilliance, and total ruthlessness that is characteristic of its leadership.

Even as this monograph goes to press, IS continues to reinvent itself in the face of awakening opposition from the West. Its intention to capture the world for Islam is the focal point of its existence. The threat of IS to the West is, therefore, both significant and imminent. IS has declared itself ready and willing to do whatever is necessary to destroy our Western principles dedicated to a celebration of life, individual freedom, a Judeo-Christian culture, government by consent of the governed, equality for all under man-made law, our history, and our future. It intends instead to force us all back into its 7th century shariah-dominated system.

As IS continues its accelerating global rampage, the end of this story is still unknown. This monograph is therefore only an introduction to IS, necessarily incomplete, as it waits for history to reveal itself. It is written for those who follow the developments and acknowledge that an understanding of the enemy is the first step to defeating it.

This monograph will define the enemy, show how it operates, and explain the threat as it is today and as it is likely to be in the near future. It is a bookmark in history unfolding.

What's in a Name?

The Islamic State is an organization that has worn many names. Currently there is wide disagreement about what it should be called. A successor group to Abu Musab al- Zarqawi's al-Qa'eda in Iraq force of the 2000s, it later became known as The Islamic State in Iraq and al-Sham (ISIS). The Arabic language acronym for ISIS is Da'esh (داعش dā'ish, derived from its Arabic name, ad-Dawlah al-Islāmiyah fī 'l- 'Irāq wa-al-Shām). Since June 2014, it has called itself simply the Islamic State. Others, including the Obama administration, refuse to refer to it as the Islamic State, and instead call it "ISIL," referring to it as the "Islamic State in the Levant."[4]

For the purposes of this study, given that the group has effectively erased earlier colonial borders that defined the artificial constructs of the 1916 Sykes-Picot Agreement in the former Iraq and Syria, and governs in many ways as a state, it will be referred to as it calls itself: the Islamic State (IS) or the Caliphate.

---

[4] The Levant, or al-Sham – aka Greater Syria - refers to the countries situated along entire southeastern shore of the Mediterranean Sea, beginning with modern-day Turkey and extending southwest all the way to Egypt, including Lebanon and Israel. This geographical and historical expanse skirts inland to the north of the Arabian Peninsula.

PART I:
THE HISTORY OF THE ISLAMIC STATE

The Islamic State is a phenomenon of the twenty-first century that harkens back to the original Caliphates, dating back to the earliest years of Islam. Taking advantage of the vacuum created by the weak policies of the West and the unwillingness of Western leadership to engage against it, the Islamic State of Iraq (ISI - precursor of IS) moved into Syria, where it joined the fight against the Asaad government, then swept back into Iraq and thrived. IS fighters cut a swath of wanton destruction, suffering, and death, leaving behind them a trail of misery and despair as they continue to surge across the Middle East and North Africa. The willingness of IS to engage in the worst brutality commanded by Islamic Law and exemplified by Muhammad himself is nothing less than jihad as practiced throughout Islamic history (except when it was suppressed by even more powerful opponents).

Wherever it has taken control, IS has changed the very character of the region. Populations have been decimated, national treasures have been destroyed, women and children have been brutalized and sold into sexual slavery, and countless non-combatants, including women and children, have been slaughtered. In late 2015, thousands of IS fighters and supporters, equipped with counterfeit Syrian passports, infiltrated the waves of mostly male, mostly Muslim migrants from all over the Islamic world who are emulating Muhammad's original hijrah from Mecca to Medina in a modern-day invasion of Europe. The young IS fighters have already begun to leave an indelible mark that is likely to permanently change the character of the nations of Europe.[5]

Since the massive flood of migrants began pouring into Europe, sexual assaults by Muslim males against European women and children have become commonplace[6] and the inability of European governments to cope with all of the problems relating to the huge Islamic invasion has become abundantly clear.

In late 2015 and early 2016, members of the EU began to reintroduce internal border controls, as the reality of unregulated mass immigration, with its unknown numbers of embedded terrorists, began to overwhelm them. The Paris attacks of November 13, 2015, proved that IS had indeed used the immigration of Syrian refugees to move its fighters into Europe, had activated groups inside the EU, and was capable of well-planned, coordinated attacks from inside the member nations. Then, four months later on March 22, 2016, a team of IS jihadis in Belgium killed 35 people and wounded over 300 others in attacks at Zaventem airport and a Brussels metro station. And although IS' presence had only barely been felt in America, experts agree that it is only a matter of time before Americans will experience similar attacks in our own cities.[7]

IS made clear the purpose of these attacks in an announcement[8] they released shortly after the Belgium attacks, in which it warned the West of more to come, and explained why the world's criticism of its killing "innocents" doesn't apply:

> *"We promised the crusader countries who have a coalition against the Islamic State black days as a response to their aggression*

---

[5] "German spy agency says ISIS sending fighters disguised as refugees." Reporting by Caroline Copley; Editing by Tom Heneghan. Reuters, February 5, 2016.
http://www.reuters.com/article/U.S.-germany-security-idU.S.KCN0VE0XL

[6] "It's not only Germany that covers up mass sex attacks by migrant men ... Sweden's record is shameful" by Ivar Arpi. *The Spectator.* January 16, 2016.
http://www.spectator.co.uk/2016/01/its-not-only-germany-that-covers-up-mass-sex-attacks-by-migrant-men-swedens-record-is-shameful/

[7] Marine Lt. Gen. Vincent Stewart, director of the Defense Intelligence Agency told the Senate Armed Services Committee that ISIS will attempt to strike U.S. targets this year.
http://www.worldmag.com/2016/02/ISIS_is_determined_to_attack_the_u_s_in_2016

[8] "ISIS warns UK to expect even 'harder and more bitter' terror atrocity than Brussels" by Sam Adams and Richard Wheatstone. *Mirror,* March 22, 2016.
http://www.mirror.co.uk/news/world-news/isis-warns-uk-expect-even-7609382

against the country of Islam. What is coming will be more catastrophic and more bitter with the permission of Allah."

In a longer statement they clarified their reasons:

> *"First we want to make it clear to all that what makes the kafir's blood permissiable [sic] to spill is not him fighting the Muslims, rather it is his "KUFR" [unbelief] that necessitates his killing. So if one asks, can you kill a Kafir (who does not fight Islam and muslims)? the answer is a big YES. ...*

> *"Allah also has made the blood of every kafir legal to spill in the general ayah: "So when the sacred months have passed away, then slay the idolaters wherever you find them, and take them captives and besiege them and lie in wait for them in every ambush" (At-Tawbah verse 5).*

> *"Allah just said the mushrikeen (idolaters), so he never differentiated the "innocent civilians" from the "fighting soldiers." So who are we to differentiate the kuffar today?"*[9]

---

[9] "In Statement Proclaiming Civilian Slaughter Halal, Islamic State Takes Credit for Brussels Attacks" by John Hayward. Breitbart.com, March 22, 2016. http://www.breitbart.com/national-security/2016/03/22/isis-claims-responsibility-for-brussels-attacks-quotes-islamic-law-to-justify-slaughter-of-civilians/

BREAKING NEWS Statement on the Blessed Brussels Raid against Crusader Belgium

Belgium   *12 Jumada al-Akhirah 1437*

By Allah's grace, a security team of the Khilafah, may Allah grant it glory and victory, set out to target crusader Belgium, which has not ceased to wage war against Islam and its people.

Allah enabled our brothers and cast fear and terror into the hearts of the crusaders deep in their own lands, where several soldiers of the Khilafah went forth, wearing explosive belts, carrying explosive devices, and armed with automatic rifles, towards specially selected locations in Brussels, the capital of Belgium.

They stormed the airport of Brussels and a metro station, killing a number of crusaders before detonating their explosive belts amid crowds of the disbelievers. The attacks resulted in the killing of more than 40 and wounding of more than 210 citizens of crusader nations, and all praise is due to Allah.

We promise black days for all crusader nations allied in their war against the Islamic State, in response to their aggressions against it, and what is to come will be more devastating and bitter by Allah's permission. Praise is due to Allah for His support and facilitation, and we ask Him to accept our brothers among the shuhada'.

In short, IS does not need to justify its attacks on what the West calls "innocents" because in Islamic terms, only Muslims can be truly innocent (all the rest being guilty for having rejected Islam). A Twitter post by Tim Ramadan[10] on March 22 shows a photo of an announcement of the Belgium attacks, purportedly produced by IS, which appeared in several languages, including English and French.

In the last paragraph, where it refers to "all crusader nations," IS has included Europe and the U.S., which they link to the Christian crusaders of the Middle Ages. This rationale disregards over 300 years of Islamic attacks against Middle East Christians and Europe itself that preceded the Crusades. That IS has included the U.S. in their calculations, where Islam has never had

---

[10] *Nom de plume* for member of "Member of #Raqqa Is being Slaughtered silently #RBSS

a ruling presence, has been made very clear as it continues to threaten America with graphic videos and incendiary statements. In order to understand how serious a threat IS poses to America, it is essential to know something about its history and how it operates in the places it has conquered.

THE BEGINNINGS – A BRIEF HISTORY OF THE ISLAMIC STATE

The Legacy of Abu Musab al-Al-Zarqawi

IS evolved over a period of years from a small group of al-Qa'eda-sponsored terrorists, led by Jordanian terrorist Abu Musab al-Al-Zarqawi. He founded the group in 1999 as Jamaat al-Tawhid wa-i-Jihad al-Qa'eda, sanctioned by bin Laden himself. Al-Zarqawi was thought to be responsible for a string of terrorist attacks in Iraq and, on November 10, 2005, for three coordinated hotel bombings in Amman, Jordan that killed 50 people and wounded 110. In February 2006, the FBI offered a $5 million bounty for his capture. Then, on June 8, 2006, Al-Zarqawi was killed by a U.S. airstrike on his safe house. (For a full biography, see Appendix I)

In October 2006, the Mujahideen Shura Council[11] established *ad-Dawlah al-'Irāq al-Islāmiyah*, also known as the Islamic State of Iraq (ISI).[12] The leadership of ISI was taken over by Abu Ayyub al-Masri and Abu Omar al-Baghdadi. Al-Masri was reportedly hand-picked by al-Qa'eda's new leader, Ayman al-Zawahiri, but very little is known about al-Baghdadi. At one time, the U.S. military released information that he was, in fact, an imaginary figure, played by an actor, but in 2007, Haditha (Iraq) police chief, Col. Fareq al Je'eify, told the news outlet *al Arabiya* that Baghdadi was an officer in the Iraqi security services who had been dismissed from the army because of his "extremism."[13]

---

[11] The Mujahideen Shura Council was founded in 2005 and served as an umbrella organization for at least six Sunni Islamic groups involved in the Iraqi insurgency: al-Qa'eda in Iraq, Jeish al-Taiifa al-Mansoura, Katbiyan Ansar Al-Tawhid wal Sunnah, Saray al-Jihad Group, al-Ghuraba Brigades, and al-Ahwal Brigades.

[12] "The Rump Islamic Emirate of Iraq" by Bill Roggio. LongWarJournal.org, October 16, 2006. http://www.longwarjournal.org/archives/2006/10/the_rump_islamic_emi.php

[13] Report: "True Identity of 'Islamic State of Iraq' Leader Revealed, Photos Aired," CBSNews.com from Al Arabiya TV. http://www.cbsnews.com/news/report-true-identity-of-islamic-state-of-iraq-leader-revealed-photos-aired/

Both al-Masri and al-Baghdadi were killed in a nighttime raid on the ISI leaders' safe-house in 2010.[14] They were succeeded by Abu Bakr al-Baghdadi, who later declared himself Caliph and brought IS to its current position of explosive growth and power.

THE SYRIAN 'CIVIL' WAR

The Syrian civil war created a perfect opening for ISI to expand its operations and to consolidate its power. The triggering event for the onset of the war occurred in March 2011 when several children in the small town of Dara'a in southern Syria were arrested and tortured by Bashar al-Assad's police for writing the anti-government graffiti "The people want to topple the regime" on a wall.[15] The news of their arrest and torture sparked a local demonstration that quickly spread into large anti-regime protests throughout the country.

As the demonstrations proliferated and al-Assad's response became increasingly repressive, it did not take long for violence and then war to

Kurdish woman tied to a pillar in Aleppo, Syria, and left with a note at her feet encouraging passersby to spit on her.

erupt. The escalating conflict spawned many small terrorist groups and drew jihadis from all over the world into Syria. The number of "rebel" groups proliferated throughout Syria. It was an opportunity ISI could not resist.

---

[14] "U.S. and Iraqi forces kill Al Masri and Baghdadi, al-Qa'eda in Iraq's top two leaders" by Bill Roggio. *The Long War Journal*, April 19, 2010.
http://www.longwarjournal.org/archives/2010/04/al_qaeda_in_iraqs_to.php
[15] "Daraa: The spark that lit the Syrian flame" by Joe Sterling, CNN. March 1, 2012.
http://www.cnn.com/2012/03/01/world/meast/syria-crisis-beginnings/index.html

While the group's original aim had been to establish an Islamic Caliphate in Iraq, the war opened the door for expansion from Iraq into Syria.

The media began disseminating photographs of civilians who had been shot *en masse* with their bodies left lying where they had fallen. The atrocities were immediately attributed to Syrian President Bashar al-Assad. The truth in fact quickly became clear that all sides were committing heinous war crimes.

"ISI began operating in Syria quietly, using the fighting of other groups as camouflage. But over time, they systematically took over large portions of northern Syria. Crimes of extreme barbarism and mass murders ... attributed to al-Assad, were clearly the work of ISI, who particularly targeted Christians, Alawites, Shia Muslims, and other minorities. Women and children were viciously tortured, raped, and murdered and men were systematically shot, beheaded, or crucified."[16] These atrocities were and still are frequently attributed to al-Assad's forces, but they were, in fact, the early hallmarks of IS. [17] Even the August 2013 gas attack on Ghouta, a suburb of Damascus, where hundreds of people were reported to have died and that has long been firmly attributed to al-Assad, was in fact carried out by al Qa'eda rebels, according to a U.N. report. The report referred specifically to "al-Nusra and its Islamist allies." Among these "allies" was the notorious ISI, later IS, which has used chlorine and mustard gas against Syrians and Kurds many times since then.[18]

As the group became increasingly involved in the Syrian war, its mission expanded to taking control of the Sunni-majority areas in northern Syria, rather than just operating there.

THE BIRTH OF THE ISLAMIC STATE

After establishing its terrorist credentials among the rebel groups in Syria, ISI began aiming for growth and the acquisition of power. In early 2013, ISI leader al-Baghdadi tried to forge a merger with Jabhat al-Nusra, al-Qa'eda's

---

[16] "Was al-Assad Responsible for the Sarin Gas Attacks in 2013? Or Was It ISIS?" by Ilana Freedman and Jerry Gordon. Freedman Report. October 2, 2014.
http://freedmanreport.com/?p=1959

[17] "Al-Qaeda Rebels Abuse and Murder Syrian Christians" by Basel Dayoub, al Akhbar - December 19, 2012. Link no longer available.

[18] "Summary of historical attacks using chemical or biological weapons," compiled by Wm. Robert Johnston. http://www.johnstonsarchive.net/terrorism/chembioattacks.html

affiliate in Syria. Although ISI and al-Nusra had frequently fought with and against each other at various times in this complicated Syrian war, they were both earlier affiliates of al-Qa'eda and a merger would have reflected ISI's expanded vision, enabling it to consolidate its gains as a precursor to establishing the Caliphate.

But ISI was moving further from the core al-Qa'eda agenda, which did not aim for the immediate establishment of the Caliphate as its primary goal. Moreover, al-Baghdadi had offended Ayman al-Zawahiri, al-Qa'eda's leader, by announcing the merger without applying to him for permission to do so. In May 2013, al-Zawahiri sent a sharp letter to both al Baghdadi and Abu Muhammad al-Julani, the leader of Jabhat al-Nusra,[19] stating very firmly that for the time being, there would be no merger, and ordering them to confine their activities to their respective fields of operations: al-Nusra in Syria and ISI in Iraq.[20]

Al-Baghdadi, however, was already committed, and responded by producing a video,[21] which he released on June 29, 2014. In the video, which was distributed online, IS spokesman Abu Mohammad al-Adnani said, "The Shura [council] of the Islamic State met and discussed [the caliphate]. ... The Islamic State decided to establish an Islamic caliphate and to designate a caliph for the state of the Muslims. ... The jihadist cleric Baghdadi was designated the caliph of the Muslims. ... The leader of Musims everywhere."[22] He said it would be called ad-Dawlah al-Islāmiyah,[23] or "Islamic State" (IS)).[24]

---

[19] "Qaeda chief annuls Syrian-Iraqi jihad merger" by Basma Atassi. *Al Jazeera,* June 9, 2013.
http://www.aljazeera.com/news/middleeast/2013/06/2013699425657882.html

[20] Analysis: Zawahiri's letter to al-Qa'eda branches in Syria, Iraq"
http://www.longwarjournal.org/archives/2013/06/analysis_alleged_let.php

[21] Ibid.

[22] "ISIS Declares Islamic Caliphate, Appoints Abu Bakr Al-Baghdadi As 'Caliph', Declares All Muslims MU.S.t Pledge Allegiance To Him" MEMRI, June 30, 2013.
http://www.memri.org/report/en/0/0/0/0/0/0/8049.htm

[23] "Iraq crisis: Isis changes name and declares its territories a new Islamic state with 'restoration of caliphate' in Middle East", by Adam Withnall. *The Independent* (London). June 29, 2014.
http://www.independent.co.uk/news/world/middle-east/isis-declares-new-islamic-state-in-middle-east-with-abu-bakr-al-baghdadi-as-emir-removing-iraq-and-9571374.html

[24] "Profile of Abu Bakr al-Baghdadi, the newly appointed 'Caliph' of 'all Muslims,' " AFP June 29, 2014. http://www.dnaindia.com/world/report-profile-of-abu-bakr-al-baghdadi-the-newly-appointed-caliph-of-all-mU.S.lims-1998592

Adnani urged Muslims to "shake off the dust of humiliation and disgrace" and "reject democracy and other garbage from the West." He said that al-Baghdadi would be the ruler of "all Muslims everywhere" and would assume the name Caliph Ibrahim. Adnani called on al-Qa'eda and Muslims around the world to pledge their allegiance to the new, self-proclaimed Caliph and to the new Caliphate.[25] It was the beginning of a period of rapid growth and power for the terrorist group.

ABU BAKR AL-BAGHDADI

Little is known about the shadowy figure of Abu Bakr al-Baghdadi (a *nom de guerre*), who is also known as Abu Du'a and the "Invisible Sheikh,"[26] but whose real name is Ibrahim Awad Ibrahim Ali Muhammad al-Badri al-Samarri.[27] U.S. State Department records list al-Baghdadi as born in Fallujah, Iraq, in 1971, although other

Abu Bakr al-Baghdadi

reports put his birth in the Iraqi city of Samarra, which is more likely because of his surname which, according to Middle East custom, indicates the city of his birth.[28] Al-Baghdadi is a highly-educated scholar of Islam, who holds a Ph.D. in Islamic jurisprudence and wears the black turban to signify direct descent from Muhammad.

On February 2, 2004, al-Baghdadi was arrested by U.S. forces near Fallujah and was interned in Camp Bucca near the city of Basra in southern Iraq. He was released in December 2004 as a "low level prisoner,"[29] according to State

[25] "Iraq crisis: ISIS declares its territories a new Islamic state with 'restoration of caliphate' in Middle East" by Adam Withnall. *The Independent,* June 30, 2014.
http://www.independent.co.uk/news/world/middle-east/ISIS-declares-new-islamic-state-in-middle-east-with-abu-bakr-al-baghdadi-as-emir-removing-iraq-and-9571374.html
[26] "Profile: Abu Bakr al-Baghdadi" BBC.com, 15 May 2015. http://www.bbc.com/news/world-middle-east-27801676
[27] https://www.scribd.com/fullscreen/256164952?access_key=key-oFhy4XTvPnuNMWMRlgs1&allow_share=true&escape=false&view_mode=scroll
[28] "ISIS: the inside story" by Martin Chulov, December 11, 2014.
http://www.theguardian.com/world/2014/dec/11/-sp-ISIS-the-inside-story
[29] "U.S. Actions in Iraq Fueled Rise of a Rebel". *The New York Times.* 10 AugU.S.t 2014. Retrieved 23 December 2014.

Department documents,[30] a mistake of colossal proportions as future events would make abundantly clear.

Al-Baghdadi's time at Camp Bucca was well-spent. According to Abu Ahmed, another prisoner at Camp Bucca, "We could never have all got together like this in Baghdad, or anywhere else. ... It would have been impossibly dangerous. Here, we were not only safe, but we were only a few hundred meters away from the entire al-Qaida leadership. ... He [al-Baghdadi] was respected very much by the U.S. army. If he wanted to visit people in another camp he could, but we couldn't. And all the while, a new strategy, which he was leading, was rising under their noses, and that was to build the Islamic State. If there was no American prison in Iraq, there would be no IS now. Bucca was a factory. It made us all. It built our ideology."[31]

This is not an exaggeration. In the end, many of the alumni of Camp Bucca played important roles in filling the leadership positions of IS.[32,33]

By October 2011, the State Department had recognized its mistake and posted "a reward offer of up to $10 million for information leading to the location, arrest, and conviction of Abu Bakr al-Baghdadi, leader of the terrorist organization Islamic State of Iraq and the Levant (ISIL)."[34] That year, he was named a Designated Global Terrorist under the terms of Executive Order 13224. He was also listed as a terrorist by the United Nations Security Council al-Qaida Sanctions Committee.[35] But by then, al-Baghdadi had gone underground and was well on his way to building his power base.

Within IS, al-Baghdadi is respected as a battlefield commander and tactician,[36] but to the outside world, his rigid enforcement of Islamic Law has

---

[30] "Iraq crisis: the jihadist behind the takeover of Mosul - and how America let him go" by Colin Freeman, June 11, 2014. *The Telegraph.*
http://www.telegraph.co.uk/news/worldnews/middleeast/iraq/10891700/Iraq-crisis-the-jihadist-behind-the-takeover-of-Mosul-and-how-America-let-him-go.html

[31] "ISIS: the inside story" by Martin Chulov.

[32] There is a stunning parallel between the indoctrination and consolidation of jihadi prisoners at Camp Bucca and the propagandizing that takes place in American prisons where Muslim Brotherhood-approved imams are actively and successfully proselytizing, converting, and indoctrinating non-Muslim prisoners.

[33] "Jihad in Prisons," CounterJihad.com. http://counterjihad.com/jihad-in-prison/

[34] http://www.state.gov/r/pa/prs/ps/2014/07/228989.htm

[35] "Rewards for Justice" U.S. Department of State.
https://www.rewardsforjU.S.tice.net/english/abu_dua.html#

[36] "Syria Iraq: The Islamic State militant group," BBC.com, August 2, 2014.
http://www.bbc.com/news/world-middle-east-24179084

made him a monster of gigantic proportions, one who must be stopped. He has remained elusive, however, and even his whereabouts after assuming power as Caliph are a matter for speculation.

Al-Baghdadi officially established his operational center in the city of Raqqa in northern Syria in January 2014. Located on the north bank of the Euphrates River, the city lies about 100 miles east of Aleppo and 25 miles east of Syria's largest dam. The capital of the Abbasid Caliphate between 796 and 809 CE, Raqqa was home to one of the most influential of the Islamic dynasties.[37] In modern times, al-Raqqa became the sixth largest city in Syria, relatively prosperous, with energy resources and an agricultural economy, but otherwise, was considered fairly ordinary. The city's lack of distinction, its size, its relatively secular, Sunni population, its history, and its location near energy resources, the Euphrates River, and Iraq may all have figured into the decision to choose Raqqa for IS' capital.

THE ISLAMIC STATE EXPANDS INTO IRAQ

IS was already beginning to feel the full flush of its successes in Syria when it opened a second front in Iraq in early 2014. Smashing their way southward through city after city, IS fighters captured a huge area in the largely Sunni parts of northern Iraq. Chief among their tactics were attacks on the Syrian border to blur, and ultimately obliterate, the artificial boundaries between Syria and Iraq, imposed by the Sykes-Picot Agreement in 1916.[38]

One of the most dramatic events, which caught the attention of the world as IS smashed its way from Syria through northern Iraq, was its capture of the Iraqi city of Mosul in early June 2014. This was the turning point in IS' economic and military fortunes.

Prior to the summer of 2014, IS had suffered from a severe shortage of weapons as they faced the U.S.-equipped Iraqi military forces, but on June 10, 2014, the day they launched their assault on Mosul, the situation changed dramatically. The Iraqi military had 30,000 soldiers stationed in Mosul. But in the face of just 1,000 IS fighters coming into the city, they fled, leaving their weapons behind and their armories unsecured. As IS overran the city,

---

[37] "The Abbasid Dynasty: The Golden Age of Islamic Civilization," published by the Saylor Foundation. Saylor.org/history101

[38] "Britain and France conclude Sykes-Picot agreement," History.com. http://www.history.com/this-day-in-history/britain-and-france-conclude-sykes-picot-agreement

they sacked the Central Bank and made off with $42 million worth of gold bullion and cash. This made IS the richest terrorist group in the world. The small IS army also attacked police stations and security posts. Its fighters helped themselves to huge stores of U.S. weaponry and vehicles, including a fleet of 2,300 Humvees valued at $1 billion, 40 M1A1 main battle tanks, 74,000 machine guns, and 52 M198 Howitzer mobile gun systems that had been left behind for the Iraqi military by departing U.S. troops.[39] By June 29, when al-Baghdadi declared his caliphate, IS had much to celebrate. The capture of Mosul had changed everything.

IS continued its conquest south into Iraq in long columns of stolen Humvees that were also seen on the roads in places like Aleppo, Syria, 250 miles away, filled with well-armed IS fighters. Although they were a prime target for an American air strike, the long columns were left to proceed unimpeded. Many consider this the single most egregious error that the U.S. made in the early days of IS' conquest – that they could have stopped IS in its tracks and didn't.

As a result, IS was able to take over large portions of Iraq and Syria, leaving a trail of sexual slavery, theft, extortion, destruction, and genocide in its wake. The terrorist group that the President Barrack Obama had dismissed as "the JV (Junior Varsity) team" had quickly become the fastest growing and wealthiest terrorist organization in the world.

THE IS CALIPHATE

Governance: Secret Files Show the Structure and Strategy of IS

Two of the most significant factors distinguishing IS from other 21st century jihadist organizations are 1) the conquest and appropriation of land from which to declare its "Caliphate" and 2) the establishment of quasi-government "agencies" to carry out the day-to-day operations.

In January 2014, Samir Abd Muhammad al-Khlifawi was killed in Syria after a brief firefight in the town of Tal Rifaat, but the rebels who shot him did not know they had killed the man known as Haji Bakr, the strategic head of IS. They also did not know that he had left behind confidential "blueprints" for IS's organizational strategy – its plans for organizing and subjugating the territories they planned to

---

[39] "ISIS Has $1B Worth Of U.S. Humvee Armored Vehicles; One Was used In Monday's Suicide Bombing Near Baghdad" by Angelo Young. *International Business Times,* January 6, 2015. http://www.ibtimes.com/ISIS-has-1b-worth-U.S.-humvee-armored-vehicles-one-was-U.S.ed-mondays-suicide-bombing-1946521

capture. *Der Spiegel*, Germany's largest news magazine, got exclusive access to those plans.[40]

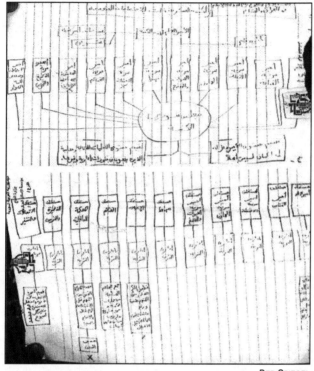

"Bakr's documents were long hidden in a tiny addition to a house in embattled northern Syria. Reports of their existence were first made by an eyewitness who had seen them in Haji Bakr's house shortly after his death. In April 2014, a single page from the file was smuggled to Turkey, where *Der Spiegel* was able to examine it for the first time. It only became possible to reach Tal Rifaat to evaluate the entire set of handwritten papers in November 2014."[41]

A page from Bakr's notes on the organization of IS

Bakr was a former colonel in the intelligence service of Saddam Hussein's air defense force, but the details surrounding his role in IS were always intentionally kept unclear. The papers he left behind, according to the *Der Spiegel* article, were found in a folder containing 31 pages of handwritten organizational charts, lists, and schedules. They described how IS would be organized and some of the directives that would form the organization's strategic and operational plans.

The papers also showed what role former officials in the government of ex-dictator Saddam Hussein would play in it, and, most significantly, how IS

---

[40] "The Terror Strategist: Secret Files Reveal the Structure of Islamic State" by Christof Reuter. *Der Spiegel*, Issue 17, April 18, 2015. http://www.spiegel.de/international/world/islamic-state-files-show-structure-of-Islamic-terror-group-a-1029274.html
[41] Ibid.

would accomplish its conquest of Syria. Even while IS was operating secretly in the early days of the Syrian war, the papers revealed that they were painstakingly planning the conquest of the country. According to *Der Spiegel*, the papers showed, in retrospect, that Haji Bakr's plans and instructions had been carried out meticulously. It was this attention to detail that contributed so heavily to IS' swift and comprehensive success in its conquest of northern Syria and Iraq.

Among the documents were notices, receipts, internal memos revealing petty rivalries between officials, and religious fatwas (Islamic rulings). They covered a wide range of issues, from the rape of female prisoners and the treatment of slaves, to such details as when it is permissible for a son to steal from his father in order to fund his travel to fight jihad. The documents also contain spreadsheets detailing their oil acquisition and distribution, and a blueprint for consolidating power in the regions under IS control.

Haji Bakr

Other recovered documents revealed that the training of children for combat was an early priority for IS. One 2014 text in particular clearly states the intention to train children and that children will be receiving "training on bearing light arms." It also says that "outstanding individuals" will be "selected from them for security portfolio assignments, including checkpoints, patrols."[42]

The papers attest to IS' preoccupation with the documentation of all of their activities. They reveal IS' obsession with details, systematically organizing its operations in every area it has conquered. The aim is to rebuild not only the infrastructure, but also the institutions "from roads to nurseries to hotels to marketplaces, from the Euphrates to the Tigris."[43] But they would be built

---

[42] Ibid.
[43] "The ISIS Papers: behind 'death cult' image lies a methodical bureaucracy" by Shiv Malik. *The Guardian*, December 7, 2015. http://www.theguardian.com/world/2015/dec/07/ISIS-papers-guardian-syria-iraq-bureaucracy

according to IS' strict enforcement of shariah. These rules would apply not only to territory that has been taken by IS in Iraq and Syria, but also its self-declared additions to the "state" in Africa, the Sinai Peninsula, and southern Asia.[44]

IS' Organizational Structure

A definitive analysis of IS' organizational structure is difficult to conduct, as the organization is designed to be fluid in the face of targeted attacks against its leadership, and the organizational structure is closely held. The success of targeted air strikes and special operations actions against senior IS people has also made changes in the roles of the leadership necessary. Prior to 2014, IS published annual reports in which it proudly released to the world information about their accomplishments, as if it were an international corporation. Since then, however, it has become considerably more secretive about the inner workings of their organization and particularly about the leadership.

The "Caliph," al-Baghdadi, sits at the top of the organizational pyramid. The members who fill out the pyramid are a combination of former military officers in Saddam Hussein's army and loyal IS leaders. Beneath Baghdadi are the following:

1. **The Military Council** is headed by Abu Ahmad al 'Alawani. The Council includes three members whose task is to plan and supervise the military commanders and the actual operations in the field. The members of the Council are all appointed by the Caliph.

2. **The Shura (Consultative) Council:** Headed by al-Amiri, who is reported to have been appointed personally by al-Baghdadi. The Shura Council is believed to include 9-11 members, all selected by Baghdadi. Abu Arkan presides over the Shura Council, the primary consultative and advisory council of IS which delivers orders from the IS leaders, al-Baghdadi and his second and third in command, Abu Ali al-Anbari and Abu Muslim al-Turkmani, respectively. The Council is responsible for supervising affairs of the state.

---

[44] "ISIS sets up departments to handle 'war spoils' including slaves, pillaged oil and stolen antiquities by Jenny Stanton. December 28, 2015. http://www.dailymail.co.uk/news/article-3376067/ISIS-sets-departments-handle-war-spoils-including-slaves-pillaged-oil-stolen-antiquities-documents-revealed-special-forces-reveal.html

3. **The Judicial Authority**: Headed by Abu Mohammad al-Ani, the Authority deals with all judicial issues as well as spreading the message of the Islamic State by means of recruitment and preaching.

4. **The Defense, Security and Intelligence Council**: This Council may be the most important at this moment, as it is not only responsible for the personal security and safety of the Caliph, but also serves to implement orders, campaigns, judicial decisions and, of course, as the agency responsible for the collection and dissemination of intelligence. This Council is headed by Abu Bakr (AKA Abu Ali) al-Anbari, a former major-general in Saddam Hussein's army together with three other high-ranking officers who served also during Saddam Hussein's rule.

5. **The Islamic State Institution for Public Information**: Headed by Abu Al Athir Omru al Abbassi. The Islamic State spokesman was Abu Mohammad al-'Adnani, who was killed in a military raid and who may have been replaced by Abu Ahmad al 'Alawani.[45]

The following chart lists some of the leading members of IS and the positions they are believed to hold. They are known by their *noms de guerre,* but very little more is known about most of them.

---

[45] See more at: http://jcpa.org/structure-of-the-islamic-state/#sthash.6JMmXNhL.dpuf

Islamic State Leadership

NOTE: This chart was considered correct as of March 2016. With the continuing loss of leadership from targeted attacks, however, some of the individuals in leadership positions may have been killed and replaced since it was compiled.

Title	Nom de Guerre / Real Name	Notes
Caliph Ibrahim, Leader of IS	Abu Bakr al-Baghdadi Real name: Ibrahim Awwad Ali al-Badri al-Samarrai	Iraqi national from the Al-Bu Badri tribe. Claims to be descendant of Mohammed
Second-in-Command to IS leader Abu Bakr al-Baghdadi.	Abu Muslim al-Turkmani Real name: Fadl Ahmad Abdullah al-Hiyali	Former Lieutenant Colonel in the Iraqi Army and a former officer in the Iraqi Special Forces from Ninewa, Iraq
	Abu Bakr al-Afari (killed) Real name: Abdul Rahman Mustafa al- Qaduli. Also known as Haji Imam, Abu Ali al-Anbari, and Abu Abd al-Rahman al-Afri	Iraqi who joined al Qaeda in 2004, worked with Al-Zarqawi. Joined up with al-Baghdadi in 2014. Reports directly to al-Baghdadi. Unconfirmed report he was killed in air-attack that also injured Baghdadi in May 2015 was false. Also head of finance for IS. *Reported killed Dec. 2015. Confirmed killed in Syria by U.S. SpecOps forces, March 24, 2016.*
Deputy for Iraq (Dawlat al-Iraq)	Abu Muslim al-Turkmani Real name: Fadl Ahmad Abdullah al-Hijali	Former Lieutenant Colonel in the Iraqi Army under Saddam Hussein and a former officer in the Iraqi Special Forces from Ninewa, Iraq (see above)
IS spokesman	Abu Muhammad al-Adnani Real name: Taha Sobhi Falaha	IS' director of external operations and media spokesman for IS, the leading voice for the dissemination of official messages. A Syrian national; pledged allegiance to Abu Musab al-Zarqawi in 2002. Reportedly injured in U.S. air strike in January 2016 in Anbar province, Iraq. Rumored to be heir-apparent to al-Baghdadi.

Title	Nom de Guerre / Real Name	Notes
Deputy for Syria **(Dawlat al-Sham)**	**Abu Ali al-Anbari** Real name: Unknown	Former Major General in the Iraqi Army under Saddam Hussein from Anbar province. Member of IS Shura Council, oversees the smaller councils that run the so-called caliphate and acts as envoy for al-Baghdadi. Also reportedly serves as head of the powerful Intelligence and Security Council and head of all military operations in Syria.
War Minister	**Abu Suleiman al-Nasser** Nasser al-Din Allah Abu Suleiman Real name: Neaman Salman Mansour al-Zaidi	Military chief and head of IS War Council. Prior to serving in IS, was War Minister of IS-predecessor Islamic State of Iraq in April 2010.
Chief of Syria military operations; (IS Defense Secretary).	**Omar al-Shishani (Omar the Chechen)** Real name: Tarkhan Tayumurazovich Batirashvili	IS commander for northern Syria and a member of the Shura Council. Ethnic Chechen/Georgian. Military strategist who is thought to have masterminded IS's rapid advances in Iraq in 2014. Designated by U.S. as Specially Designated Global Terrorist, with $5 million bounty for information leading to his capture. *Confirmed killed in U.S. air strike in Syria on March 4, 2016.*
Senior military commander	**Abu Wahib** Real name: Shaker Wahib al-Fahdawi	Arrested by U.S. forces (2006), sentenced to death. Escaped prison in September 2012.
Minister of General Management	**Abu Abd al-Kadir** Real name: Shawkat Hazm al-Farhat	
Minister of Prisoners	**Abu Mohammed** Real name: Bashar Ismail al-Hamdani	
Minister of General Security	**Abu Abdulrahman al-Bilawi** Real name: Adnan Ismael Najm	Al-Bilawi was one of the four members of the IS military council and was formerly head of the Shura

Title	Nom de Guerre / Real Name	Notes
	Replaced by al-Suwaydawi, who took his place	council. Originally from al-Khalidiya in Iraq's Anbar province, he spent time in Camp Bucca. Killed in al-Khalidiya, Anbar in June 2014.
	Haji Bakr Real Name: Samir al-Khlifawi	Haji Bakr was a colonel in Iraqi intelligence services and first leader of IS Military Council. He was killed in a clash with Syrian rebels in January 2014.
Minister of Finance	**Abu Alaa al-Afari** Real name: Abd al-Rahman Mustafa al-Qaduli. Also known as Also known as Abu Ali al-Anbari and Abu Abd al-Rahman al-Afri	Iraqi who joined al Qaeda in 2004, worked with Al-Zarqawi. Joined up with al-Baghdadi in 2014. Reports directly to al-Baghdadi. Unconfirmed report he was killed in air-attack that also injured Baghdadi in May 2015 was false. Also head of finance for IS. *Confirmed killed in Syria by U.S. SpecOps forces, March 24, 2016.*
	Abu Salah Real name: Muafaq Mustafa Mohammed al-Karmoush	One of the most senior and experienced members of the group's financial network. *Killed in U.S. airstrike, December 2015.*
Minister of General Coordination	Abu Hajjar al-Assafi Real name: Mohammed Hamid al-Dulaimi	Responsible for coordinating communications and the distribution of resources within the Islamic State.
Minister of Foreign Fighters & Suicide Bombers	Abu Kassem Real name: Abdullah Ahmad al-Mashadani	
Minister for Social Services	Abu Saji Real name: Aouf Abd al-Rahman al-Arfi	
Minister for Weapons	Abu Sima Real name: Faris Riyadh al-Nuaimi	

Title	Nom de Guerre / Real Name	Notes
Minister for Explosives	**Abu Kifah** Real name: Khairy Abd al-Hamoud al-Taiy	
Senior Facilitator & Financier	**Abu Umar** Real name: Tariq Bin al-Tahar Bin al-Falih al-Awni al-Harzi	Senior facilitator from Tunisia, responsible for recruitment of foreign fighters and collection of finance. Based in Syria.
Chief of Media Operations	**Ahmad Abousamra** (real name)	Syrian-American national who manages IS' media operations, allegedly from Aleppo.

When IS began to build "the Islamic State," it immediately distinguished itself from other terrorist groups. The process of establishing an operational, government-like structure with "departments" (*diwans*), which were assigned quasi-governmental functions, was unique. IS leaders were, in fact, building the governing body for a state, with a strict hierarchical structure and a meticulous approach to planning and record-keeping in order to manage the growing activities and populations that IS had and would acquire. IS' plans for the expansion of the "caliphate" were ambitious.

The organizational brilliance of IS can be seen in how quickly it was able to apply the detailed planning to the newly captured territories in Syria and Iraq. Upon taking over an area, it immediately installed a governing bureaucracy that applied and enforced Islamic Law.

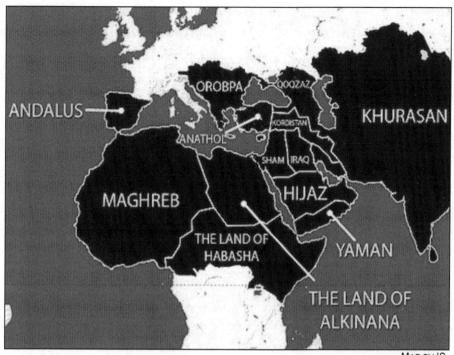

Map of the Caliphate, as imagined by IS

The map above, generated by IS to show the world its global intentions, covers all of the Middle East and North Africa, Southeast Asia (including all of the Indian sub-continent), Greece, Spain, Portugal, major parts of Russia, and a large portion of Eastern Europe. It underscores the ambitious agenda that drives IS to continue to acquire and dominate as much territory as possible to achieve its dream of a global caliphate. With certain exceptions (such as Italy), the map also reflects the farthest reach of the Islamic conquests throughout history and reminds its intended targets that, according to the Islamic doctrine of Sacred Space, any land ever conquered or occupied by Islam must be regained, even if it has subsequently slipped from its control.

As in any government, IS set up departments to run the day-to-day operations of the area, but the functions of the various departments bear little resemblance to equivalent such departments in the West. According to the captured documents, IS' tightly controlled, highly disciplined organization has centralized departments to oversee its operations under the strict shariah it has imposed on every city and town it has captured. The *diwan* responsible for Natural Resources, for example, includes in its mandates not only control over the all the oil captured, from the ground through production and sales, but also the disposition of stolen antiquities, looted from museums and ancient temples. Another *diwan* is tasked to manage "war spoils," [46] which means, to IS, the disposition of slaves, captured in the cities and villages it has conquered.

According to Abu Hamza, [47] a Syrian defector from IS' intelligence unit, selected leaders are responsible for IS's military and security forces. Civilian *diwans* are run by ministers who are responsible for their administration. Each Syrian province that IS controls is governed by an emir with both military and civilian deputies. The emirs organize and oversee the local administration of the areas under their jurisdiction. New courts, local police forces, and an extensive economic administration have been put in place, while existing education, health, telecom, and electricity systems have been completely taken over and reorganized.

The Department of Education is responsible for outlawing the teaching of certain subjects, such as music and history, while another *diwan* issues notifications, including, for example, that which called for the burning to death of Jordanian pilot Muadh al-Kasesbeh. The same department issues fatwas and monitors the compliance of Islamic shops to IS laws.

IS's strict enforcement of shariah requires that women must dress "modestly" and men must not have pictures on their T-shirts. Only women can work in women's clothing shops. Alcohol and tobacco are forbidden, and shops in areas under IS control are required to close during prayer time, so that the shopkeepers can be free to attend prayers at the local mosque. Presence at regular prayers is mandatory, and one who does not attend may face a penalty as lenient as a $20 fine and 25 lashes, or as harsh as the death penalty.

---

[46] "ISIS sets up departments to handle 'war spoils' including slaves, pillaged oil and stolen antiquities" by Jenny Stanton. *Mail OnLine, Reuters.* December 28 2015.

[47] "The anatomy of ISIS: How the 'Islamic State' is run, from oil to beheadings" by Nick Thompson and Atika Shubert, CNN. January 14, 2015
http://www.cnn.com/2014/09/18/world/meast/ISIS-syria-iraq-hierarchy/

Women in the Islamic State

Women in IS-controlled areas are subject to the harsh regulations of Islamic Law. The IS morality police, the *Hisbah*, is tasked with enforcing public morality and adherence to strict Islamic observance, meting out punishment for infractions. All women are required to wear the *niqab*, usually black, which totally covers their faces except for their eyes. Since August 2014, women also require a *mahram* (a male companion who is a close family member) to accompany them when they go out.

These, like other rules that derive from the Qur'an and shariah, are not negotiable. Adherence for women is monitored by an all-female brigade called *al-Khansa*. Men are subject to the oversight of an all-male *Hisbeh* force. Penalties for infractions of these laws are severe, up to and including stoning to death for adultery.

On 23 January 2015, the all-female Al-Khansa Brigade's "media wing" began circulating a document entitled "Women in the Islamic State: Manifesto and Case Study."[48] While the manifesto confirms that IS has all-women police brigades, and even some limited military roles for women, the primary role of women is clearly, as commanded by Allah in the Qur'an, always subservient to men, and "divinely limited" to "motherhood and family support."[49]

Because IS has a large number of followers whose native language is not Arabic, it translates much of its propaganda into languages other than Arabic, demonstrating a proficiency in targeting the specific audiences it is most interested in influencing. Significantly, this manifesto document on women has been published only in Arabic, which suggests that its target audience is the Muslim women living in IS-controlled areas, who must understand their role under IS.

The "manifesto" makes clear the direction it is taking from the outset.

> *"The era of Western dominance and its influence on our lifestyle and way of living has passed. ... The Islamic society that emerged with the establishment of the Islamic State in the lands of Iraq and Syria is a society formed, first and foremost, to worship the one*

---

[48] "Women of the Islamic State" by Charlie Winter. Quilliam, February 2015. Translation by Quilliam. http://www.quilliamfoundation.org/wp/wp-content/uploads/publications/free/women-of-the-islamic-state3.pdf
[49] Ibid.

and only God [Allah]. Everything that conflicts with this purpose is bound to Hell."

To emphasize its importance, this appears on the first page of the introduction, quickly followed by:

"Foremost among the first people that we refer to are Muslim women, members of their Islamic community. In that day, they had a role. Today, too, they have a role, one which is derived from the principles of Islamic law and its teachings."

The document includes guidelines for exceptions to these strict constraints, when a woman may be permitted to go "outside":

Women may go out to serve the community in a number of situations, the most important being:

1) Jihad (by appointment) – if the enemy is attacking her country and the men are not enough to protect it and the imams give a fatwa for it, as the blessed women of Iraq and Chechnya did, with great sadness, if the men are absent even they are present.

2) The most common reason is for studying the sciences of religion.

3) Female doctors or teachers may leave, but they must keep strictly to shariah guidelines.

It is always preferable for a woman to remain hidden and veiled, to maintain society from behind this veil. This, which is always the most difficult role, is akin to that of a director, the most important person in a media production, who is behind the scenes organizing.[50]

---

[50] Ibid.

Part II:
Funding the Islamic State

ACQUISITION OF WEALTH

One of the most stunning developments for IS has been its rapid accumulation of wealth. As with many new ventures, IS began its ascendency with the investment of like-minded, high value donors. According to a CFR report,[51] it is believed that supporters in Jordan, Syria, and Saudi Arabia provided early funding for the terrorist group. Since then, IS has become the wealthiest terrorist organization in the world, with an estimated revenue stream of $2 billion a year.[52] The U.S. State Department estimates that it may have raised over $1 billion in 2014, its first year of operation as IS.[53]

There is no official accounting of how many weapons IS acquired in the early days of its military advances, but the numbers seem to be huge. Ahmad Dabaash, spokesman for the Islamic Army quipped, "Praise God, we soon had enough weapons to fight for one or two years!" [54]

IS has enriched itself through the identification and exploitation of the "assets" it has acquired. Its methods are both brutal and illegal under international law (but not shariah). Assets include stolen money, gold, weapons, factories and farms, "taxes," slaves, and looted antiquities. In 2015, for example, IS took in $1.3 billion from a variety of sources, including $300

---

[51] "Backgrounder: The Islamic State" by Zachary Laub and Jonathan Masters. November 16, 2015. http://www.cfr.org/iraq/islamic-state/p14811

[52] How did ISIS become the richest terror organization in the world?" by Rachel Avraham. Jerusalem Online. November 16, 2015 http://www.jerU.S.alemonline.com/news/middle-east/the-arab-world/how-did-ISIS-become-the-richest-terror-organization-in-the-world-17169

[53] "Documenting ISIL's Antiquities Trafficking: The Looting and Destruction of Iraqi and Syrian Cultural Heritage: What We Know and What Can Be Done," September 29, 2015. Remarks by Andrew Keller, Deputy Assistant Secretary for Counter Threat Finance and Sanctions, Bureau of Economic and Business Affairs, U.S. Department of State. http://www.state.gov/e/eb/rls/rm/2015/247610.htm

[54] "ISIS weapons windfall may alter balance in Iraq, Syria conflicts" by Nabih Bulos, Patrick J. McDonnell and Raja Abdulrahim. ww.latimes.com/world/middleeast/la-fg-iraq-ISIS-arms-20140629-story.html#page=1

million from taxes (extortion), $160 million from "farming," and $80 million from the theft of stolen art and looted antiquities.[55]

MOSUL – A GREAT LEAP FORWARD

Prior to the capture of Mosul, IS was thought to have assets of some $900 million, but after the fall of Mosul, IS' net worth shot up to more than $2 billion, according to Professor Peter Neumann of King's College London.[56] When Iraqi soldiers fled the Central Bank in Mosul and abandoned their U.S.-provided weapons and vehicles,[57] the terrorists walked off with $429 million, much of it in gold bullion, and well over a billion dollars' worth of U.S. Army vehicles and weapons.[58]

On June 11, 2014, in an alarming turn of events, it was reported[59] that IS had overrun the Saddam Hussein-era al-Muthanna chemical weapons (CW) complex 60 miles north of Baghdad. This coup gave them access to hundreds of tons of potentially deadly CW agents, including mustard and sarin gas. Although U.S. and UN sources said at the time that the agents were so degraded that it would be impossible to weaponize them,[60] it can be argued that these materials could still be lethal in other than "weaponized" form.

OIL REVENUES

IS took control of most of Syria's oil fields, and until the end of 2015, crude oil was the group's biggest single source of revenue, providing approximately $1.57 million per day.[61] The U.S. Treasury Department estimates that up until December 2015, IS was earning around $500 million a year from selling discounted oil on the black market. Since the beginning of

[55] "Security and Defense: A decisive year for ISIS" by Yaakov Lappin. *Jerusalem Post,* January 30, 2016. http://www.jpost.com/Middle-East/Security-and-defense-A-decisive-year-for-IS-443186
[56] "Syria Iraq: The Islamic State militant group." BBC.com AugU.S.t 2, 2014. http://www.bbc.com/news/world-middle-east-24179084
[57] "ISIS Has $1B Worth Of U.S. Humvee Armored Vehicles" by Angelo Young. *International Business Times,* June 1, 2015. http://www.ibtimes.com/ISIS-has-1b-worth-U.S.-humvee-armored-vehicles-one-was-U.S.ed-mondays-suicide-bombing-1946521
[58] Ibid.
[59] "ISIS storms Saddam-era chemical weapons complex in Iraq" by Damien McElroy. *The Telegraph.* June 19, 2014. http://www.telegraph.co.uk/news/worldnews/middleeast/iraq/10913275/ISIS-storms-Saddam-era-chemical-weapons-complex-in-Iraq.html
[60] "Iraq confirms rebels seized Muthanna chemical arms site" BBC News. July 9, 2014.
[61] "Inside ISIS Inc.: The journey of a barrel of oil." By Erika Solomon, Robin Kwong and Steven Bernard. Financial Times. December 11, 2015 http://ig.ft.com/sites/2015/ISIS-oil/

persistent coalition air strikes on oil producing facilities and distribution channels, revenues from oil has diminished significantly from what it was until then.

IS was reportedly selling much of its oil to privately-owned refineries that sprang up near the little pumps that dot the landscape in Syria. Owned and operated by civilians who are unaffiliated with Islamic State, they take the crude oil directly from the ground, refine it into an inferior but saleable product, and sell it to a black market happy to take it off their hands. These civilians have suffered greatly from the air campaign against IS' oil infrastructure.

In an illustrated article in the *Financial Times* dated December 11, 2015, the authors wrote, "Though many believe that IS relies on exports for its oil revenue, it profits from its captive markets closer to home in the rebel-held territories of northern Syria and in its self-proclaimed "caliphate", which straddles the border between Syria and Iraq.

"The group sells most of its crude directly to independent traders at the oil fields. In a highly organized system, Syrian and Iraqi buyers go directly to the oil fields with their trucks to buy crude. This used to result in them waiting for weeks in traffic jams that sprawled for miles outside of oilfields. But since airstrikes against oil vehicles intensified, IS revamped its collection system. Now, when truckers register outside the field and pick up their number in line, they say they are told exactly what time they can return to fill up to avoid a pile-up of vehicles and make a more obvious target for strikes."[62]

Other customers included local petrol stations and power companies. Among the most lucrative customers for this oil, however, were the Al-Assad government and Turkey,[63] America's "ally", which is apparently playing both sides in the ongoing conflict. According to an article in the Los Angeles Times dated December 6, 2015, Russia accused Turkey's president, Recep Tayyip Erdogan, of colluding with IS in an "industrial-scale, illegal oil trade." They reported the claims of Russia's Deputy Defense Minister

[62] Ibid.

[63] "Russia says Turkish president benefits from ISIS oil trade," Fox News Service, December 2, 2015. http://www.foxnews.com/world/2015/12/02/rU.S.sia-says-turkish-president-benefits-from-ISIS-oil-trade/

Anatoly Antonov, that "the main customer for this oil stolen from Syria and Iraq is Turkey."[64]

Months of U.S. bombing raids did relatively little to cut off the oil revenues. The Obama administration claimed that concern about killing civilian drivers of the oil tankers prevented them from bombing them at all. In the face of British and French actions in December 2015, however, the U.S. Air Force joined the assault on IS oil revenues. It began to target the long lines of oil tankers, although, following the example of Israel's Air Force in Gaza, they dropped leaflets on the convoys, urging the drivers to flee their trucks before the bombing that would undoubtedly kill them.[65]

Although oil has been an extremely lucrative revenue source for the IS machine, it is not the only source of revenue for the terrorists. It is not even the most profitable.

EXTORTION ('TAXES') AND THEFT

The systematic extortion from the populations wherever IS takes control represents far and away the most profitable source of ongoing revenues for the terrorists. Early on, IS instituted a robust system of taxation on all the people living in the areas it conquered. It is based on the Islamic system of *zakat*[66], one of the Five Pillars of Islam, which requires Muslim individuals and businesses to hand over a fixed annual percentage of their assets to Islam and dates back to the days of Mohammed.

IS demands 2.5% of net worth, annually, from both individuals and businesses. Physicians, who are forced to provide volunteer service at area hospitals at least one day a week, are assessed according to days served. Even the salaries of Iraqi government officials cannot escape the IS taxman. Mosul officials paid $23 million in taxes on their salaries (although they

---

[64] "How does Islamic State make money off oil fields in Syria and Iraq?" by Nabih Bulos. *Los Angeles Times*, December 6, 2015. http://www.latimes.com/world/middleeast/la-fg-islamic-state-oil-qa-20151206-story.html

[65] "U.S. launch airstrikes on ISIS oil trucks which generate millions of pounds for jihadis" by Peter Henn. *The Express*, November 17, 2015.
http://www.express.co.uk/news/world/619922/ISIS-oil-lorries-bombed

[66] *Zaqat* is the mandatory annual tax on a certain portion of one's wealth to be distributed according to a strict 8-part division of recipients, one of which is jihad. It is considered one of the obligatory Five Pillars of Islamic religious practice.

received them from the Iraqi government) for almost a year after the city was overrun by IS.[67]

As the Muslim troops move inexorably from town to city to town, they demand *zakat*[68] from local businesses. It is collected several times a month from small shopkeepers and large businesses alike. From this oppressive tactic, it is estimated that they have been able to net more than $8 million a month.

Under IS, *zakat* is a euphemism for protection money. For the residents, the choice of whether or not to pay the "taxes" is simple. Failure to comply with these extortion efforts, or even failure to pay on time can result in penalties that include murder, kidnapping, and loss and/or the destruction of their property. IS' reputation for unspeakable brutality keeps their victims in line. All commercial activities (and many private individuals) in the areas controlled by IS are, without exception, subject to IS' extortion demands.[69]

Raqqa is a model for IS's system of taxation. According to an American reporter, "Shopkeepers from Raqqa I talked to in southern Turkey told me the group takes 2.5 percent of their revenue, deemed *zakat*, the alms payment in Islam, and a monthly fee of 1,500 Syrian pounds (SYP), or roughly $8.30; it is never described as a tax. IS now collects around 400 SYP per month for telephone lines, even though the costs are borne by the al-Assad regime. Locals also report that salaries are regularly paid to both civilian workers and fighters, who get $400 or more per month. Under the guise of consumer protection, IS regulates the price and quality of goods."[70]

[67] "U.S. airstrike in Mosul blows up 'millions' in ISIS cash," Fox News, January 11, 2016. Jennifer Griffin contributed to this report. http://www.foxnews.com/world/2016/01/11/U.S.-airstrike-in-mosul-blows-up-millions-in-ISIS-cash.html

[68] According to the *'Umdat al-Salik* or Reliance of the Traveller: A Classic Manual of Islamic Sacred Law certified in 1991 by Al-Azhar University & other senior Islamic authorities, Zakat 'is a particular amount of property that must be payed to certain kinds of recipients under the conditions specified...' *Zakat* is obligatory and one of the Five Pillars of Islam; it is never a voluntary contribution to help the poor, but as with those under the control of IS, it is a mandatory tax or protection money that helps to fund further jihad.

[69] "The ISIS Economy: Crushing Taxes and High Unemployment" by Joanna Paraszczuk. *The Atlantic,* September 2, 2015. http://www.theatlantic.com/international/archive/2015/09/ISIS-territory-taxes-recruitment-syria/403426/

[70] How ISIS Rules by Sarah Birke, *The New York Review of Books,* February 5, 2015. http://www.nybooks.com/articles/2015/02/05/how-ISIS-rules/

REVENUES FROM THE LAND

Often overlooked in the long list of IS atrocities is its theft of fertile farm land in Syria and Iraq. IS takes 5 percent of irrigated crops and 10 percent of rain-fed crops from farmers,[71] and is reported to have seized as much as $200 million in wheat from the storage silos of Iraqi farmers. The area that once was the breadbasket of the region, providing approximately half of Syria's wheat, about a third of Iraq's wheat, and nearly 40 percent of Iraq's barley,[72] is now lost. The fields, which had the potential of yielding $200 million per year for the farmers if the crops were harvested and sold, are now controlled by the terrorists.

In a *Financial Times* report[73], estimates that were provided by both Iraqi officials and Syrian farmers suggest that $20 million worth of *zakat* was collected on grain and cotton by IS. "Iraqi farmers contacted by the FT said they paid *zakat* in livestock and crops, while in Syria farmers report that many IS tax collectors calculate market prices and ask for the cash equivalent." Trucks traveling into IS territory are charged customs duties totaling up to about $140 million a year.

LOOTING AND BLACK MARKET SALE OF STOLEN ART AND ANTIQUITIES

The next most fruitful source of revenue is the plundering and sale of ancient artifacts from Syria and Iraq, stolen from museums and from ancient sites before blowing them up and destroying them forever. The rate at which IS has been plundering and destroying ancient sites is "unprecedented"[74] and has stripped the world of some of its most valuable historical treasures.

---

[71] "U.S. airstrike in Mosul blows up 'millions' in ISIS cash," Fox News, January 11, 2016. Jennifer Griffin contributed to this report. http://www.foxnews.com/world/2016/01/11/U.S.-airstrike-in-mosul-blows-up-millions-in-ISIS-cash.html

[72] This is according to UN agricultural officials and an unnamed Syrian economist, as reported in "Why U.S. Efforts to Cut Off Islamic State's Funds Have Failed" by Cam Simpson and Matthew Philips. *Bloomberg Business,* November 19, 2015.
http://www.bloomberg.com/news/articles/2015-11-19/why-u-s-efforts-to-cut-off-islamic-state-s-funds-have-failed

[73] "ISIS Inc.: Loot and taxes keep jihadi economy churning" *The Irish Times,* January 17, 2015.
http://www.irishtimes.com/bU.S.iness/economy/ISIS-inc-loot-and-taxes-keep-jihadi-economy-churning-1.2467100

[74] "ISIS is plundering archaeological treasures at an 'unprecedented' pace" by Justine Drennan. The Week. November 12, 2014. http://theweek.com /articles/442902/ISIS-plundering-archaeological-treasures-unprecedented-pace

In March 2015, IS demolished the ancient ruins of Nimrod in Iraq, a 3,300 year-old walled city, where the Tower of Babel was believed to have been built. They also bulldozed the 2,000 year-old, fortified frontier city of Hatra. Both were UNESCO world heritage sites, and these acts of destruction were called "war crimes" by United Nations Secretary General Ban Ki-Moon. Their loss to the history of civilization is incalculable.

Among other priceless treasures destroyed by IS were ancient ruins in the city of Palmyra, another UNESCO World Heritage Site, which dates back nearly 2,000 years. As IS moved closer to the ancient city in May 2015, many feared what they might do to the world famous Roman ruins there. The city lies 150 miles northeast of Damascus and was home to some of the most exquisite artifacts of the Roman era. It had been a destination for thousands of tourists each year before the outbreak of the Syrian war. The city that UNESCO called "an irreplaceable treasure", now stood in the path of IS, and the "monumental ruins of a great city that was one of the most important cultural centers of the ancient world" was threatened with destruction.

Nimrod before its destruction by IS

IS lived up to its reputation by demolishing many of the ancient sites with hammers, drills, and explosives. Centuries of treasured architecture that had withstood the wars of marauding armies for thousands of years, were reduced to rubble in a matter of moments at the hands of IS soldiers.

Palmyra temple before its destruction

After the temple was destroyed by IS

<small>PHOTOS BY IS</small>

The Islamic State, like all Islamic armies of conquest, claims that it destroys the art, holy places, literature, and monuments of any civilization that pre-dates Islam in order to remove temptations to idolatry; but that is hardly the whole story. As Robert Spencer explains, "doing so testifies to the truth of Islam, as the Qur'an suggests that ruins are a sign of Allah's punishment of those who rejected his truth:

> *Many were the Ways of Life that have passed away before you: travel through the earth, and see what was the end of those who rejected Truth. (Qur'an 3:137)"*[75]

Further, if, as Muslims believe, all that pre-dates Islam is from a time of *jahiliyya* — barbarism and unbelief — then it has no worth in the eyes of Allah and must be obliterated as a religious obligation.

Nonetheless, IS has made a lucrative business of first stealing many of the artifacts and selling them on the black market, commanding high prices in

---

[75] Spencer, Robert, "How and Why Islam Wages War Against 'Idolatry,' " *PJ Media,* March 16, 2015. https://pjmedia.com/lifestyle/2015/03/16/how-why-islam-wages-war-against-idolatry/

the $7 billion antiquities market. Because there are currently "no restrictions on antiquities from Syria coming into the U.S., American collectors and dealers knowingly or unknowingly may be boosting the Islamic State's coffers every day,"[76] by purchasing IS's jihad booty.

An especially brutal chapter of IS' saga of destruction played out in Palmyra. Prior to the arrival of IS into Palmyra, the 81-year-old curator of the city's treasures, Khaled al-Asaad, who was considered "one of the most important pioneers in Syrian archaeology in the 20th Century", raced to hide as many of the ancient artifacts as possible. Asaad had spent over 50 years working at the UNESCO World

GETTY IMAGES
Khaled al-Asaad with ancient carvings

Heritage site, and had written many books and scientific texts on the archeological treasures in Palmyra. When IS took over the city, al-Asaad was captured and tortured for more than a month in order to force him to reveal where the treasures had been hidden. In August 2015, Asaad was beheaded and his body was hanged from a column in the town's main square.[77]

In October 2015, IS fighters bound three men to columns of the Palmyra temple with a massive amount of explosives and then murdered them as they detonated the explosives and destroyed the temple. They proudly distributed the video of their wanton destruction and brutality through the Internet.

[76] "ISIS selling Iraq's artifacts in black market: UNESCO" *al-Arabiya,* September 30, 2014. http://english.alarabiya.net/en/News/middle-east/2014/09/30/IS-selling-Iraq-s-artifacts-in-black-market.html

[77] "ISIS beheads 82-year-old archaeologist in Palmyra, Syrian official says," August 19, 2015. http://www.foxnews.com/world/2015/08/19/ISIS-reportedly-beheads-82-year-old-archaeologist-in-palmyra.html

IS PHOTO (EDITED)
IS murders and beheadings in Palmyra street

"The terrorists have killed more than 400 people and mutilated their bodies, under the pretext that they cooperated with the government and 'did not follow orders,' Syria's state news agency said. It added that dozens of those killed were state employees, including the head of nursing department at the hospital and all her family members."[78] The group also released a video in July showing some 20 captured government soldiers being shot dead at Palmyra's theatre at the hands of teen-age recruits.[79]

HUMAN TRAFFICKING

Once of IS' most lucrative sources of revenue is its well-organized system of buying and selling captured women and girls as young as 10 years old to be used as sex slaves, in keeping with Islamic Law and the example of Muhammad as recounted in the Qur'an, hadith, and *Sira* (his biography). Every city and town that IS overruns becomes a resource for IS to fill its coffers with the profits made from the sale of captive women. As throughout the history of Islamic jihad, the practice clearly plays a significant role in the IS economy.

---

[78] "Just days after seizing Palmyra, ISIS massacres 400 people in the ancient city" by Doug Bolton. *The Independent,* May 24, 2015. http://www.independent.co.uk/news/world/middle-east/jU.S.t-days-after-seizing-palmyra-ISIS-massacres-400-people-in-the-ancient-city-10272934.html

[79] "Syrian archaeologist 'killed in Palmyra' by IS militants" BBC.com, August 15, 2015. http://www.bbc.com/news/world-middle-east-33984006

Two groups have suffered unimaginably at the hands of IS: entire Christian communities with historic roots in Syria and Iraq that go back centuries, and the Yazidis, who claim to practice the oldest religion in the world.[80] For some 700 years, the Yazidis have been the targets of Muslims who claim that because of their heterodox beliefs, Yazidis are either "heretics" or worse, apostates, which (according to shariah) makes it legal to kill them. Over the past seven centuries, Yazidis claim that 23 million of their people have been murdered, which has brought the Yazidi people "to the brink of extinction." It is estimated that there are only a million Yazidis left in the world. [81]

In August 2014, IS launched an attack against the Yazidi city of Sinjar, in northern Iraq. As many as 5,000 Yazidis were murdered, and another 50,000 fled. Thousands of Yazidi women and children were captured for the sex slave market.

ARAB MEDIA

IS Slaves being forced to walk in chains

In IS' slick magazine *Dabiq* Issue 4, [82] IS' treatment of its captives is discussed at length. According to the article, the decision to take Yazidi girls and women as sex slaves was given con-siderable thought. "Prior to the taking of Sinjar, Shari'ah students in the Islamic State were tasked to research the Yazidis to determine [how] they should be treated." This is consistent with what we are learning about IS' methodical approach to their entire process of conquest and control of populations. The conclusion that these "scholars" reached was defended in the article:

---

[80] According to the Yazidi calendar, it is the year 6765. According to the Gregorian calendar, their year 6775 began on April 15, 2015. This makes the Yazidi calendar 4,750 years older than the Christian or Gregorian Calendar, 990 years older than the Jewish Calendar, and 5329 years older than the Muslim Calendar. (http://www.childrenofYazidi.org/#!history/c1g31)

[81] "The Yazidis," YazidiTruth.org. http://www.Yaziditruth.org/the_Yazidis

[82] *Dabiq*, Issue 4, available at: http://media.clarionproject.org/files/islamic-state/islamic-state-ISIS-magazine-Issue-4-the-failed-crU.S.ade.pdf

> *"After capture, the Yazidi women and children were then divided according to the Shari'a amongst the fighters of the Islamic State who participated in the Sinjar operations, after one fifth of the slaves were transferred to the Islamic State's authority. … Before Shaytān [Satan] reveals his doubts to the weak-minded and weak hearted, **one should remember that enslaving the families of the kuffār [infidels] and taking their women as concubines is a firmly established aspect of the Shari'ah.** … "*[83]

What too many in the West fail to understand is that the Islamic State takes care to adhere closely to Islamic doctrine, law, and scripture. But because so many in Western academia, government and national security leadership, and the media have spent far too little time studying either the Islamic canon or the history of the Islamic conquests, they are often shocked to learn what is completely acceptable to Muslims under shariah. IS believes that the rape of young non-Muslim girls is perfectly acceptable because Mohammed himself set the example by taking sex slaves from among conquered populations and permitting his men to do the same. Indeed, sex slavery is explicitly condoned in the Qur'an, which is considered the literal word of Allah.[84] Further, of course, underage and forced marriage is also permissible under shariah, because Muhammad is reported to have married Aisha when she was only six years old, and consummated the marriage when she turned nine (although some Islamic analysts have gone to great lengths to deny this).[85]

So in August 2014, when IS soldiers overran the Yazidi town of Sinjar, Iraq, they began killing and kidnapping thousands of men, women, and children. The women and girls were sold to IS men and foreign buyers. The fair, blonde Yazidi girls were highly prized and commanded higher prices than the darker girls.

---

[83] *Escape From Hell: Torture and Sexual Slavery in Islamic State Captivity in Iraq,* Amnesty International, Ltd. 2014. https://www.amnesty.org.uk/sites/default/files/escape_from_hell_-_torture_and_sexual_ slavery_in_islamic_state_captivity_in_iraq_-_english_0.pdf

[84] Not only is sexual slavery explicitly condoned in Qur'anic Verse 4:3, but the Assembly of Muslim Jurists of America (AMJA), which provides juridical advice to American Muslims, confirmed as recently as 2005 that the practice was acceptable. See Assembly of Muslim Jurists of America, *Fatwa ID* 22853, 'Relationship with female slaves,' 2005-08-10. http://www.amjaonline.org/fatwa-22853/info

[85] "Age of Aisha (ra) at time of marriage" compiled by Zahid Aziz. http://www.muslim.org/islam/aisha-age.htm Further, again according to the Assembly of Muslim Jurists of America, "Children also can get married at any age…" *Fatwa ID* 3382, 'In Islam has it ever mentioned a specific age limits is a must for marriage or having children?, 2007-09-08' http://www.amjaonline.org/fatwa-3382/info

According to the Qur'an and hadith, an enslaved woman is referred to as "that which your right hands possess" (*i.e.*, a non-Muslim, female slave who is "owned" by a Muslim man). The following text serves as an example (one of many) of this rationalization:

> *"Prophet, We have made lawful to you the wives to whom you have granted dowries and the slave girls whom God has given you as booty."* *(Qur'an 33:50)*

Ibn Sa'd gives additional insight into the legality of having sexual relations with female slaves, referring to Mohammed's own relations with Mariyah, a Coptic Christian slave:

> *Muhammad had sexual relations with Mariyah, his Coptic slave. Mariyah and her sister, Sirin were slaves given as gifts to Muhammad. Muhammad gave Sirin to Hasan Thabit, the poet. Ibn Sa'd says that Muhammad "liked Mariyah, who was of white complexion, with curly hair and pretty."* [Taken from Ibn Sa'd's "Kitab al-Tabaqat al-Kabir" (Book of the Major Classes), p151].[86]

IS man and his newly acquired Yazidi sex slave

---

[86] "Mohammed, Muslim, Slavery, and Islam" Slavery in Islam, by Silas. http://answering-islam.org/Silas/slavery.htm

Because the selling of captive women and girls is justified by Islamic doctrine, the practice is as common among 21st century jihadis as those of the 7th century. In a report on IS, the UN revealed that teenage girls abducted by Islamic State fighters in Iraq and Syria are being sold in slave markets "for as little as [the price of] a pack of cigarettes."[87]

An online IS magazine published the following notice: "Enslaved families are now being sold." It went on to assure its readers that "Sharia students" had reviewed the practice for its "legality."[88]

Rose George wrote a sad and moving epitaph to Sinjar and to the thousands of Yazidis, now dispersed, enslaved, or dead, who had lived there. "Yazidis no longer live in the town of Sinjar, because there is hardly any Sinjar left to live in. When IS forces invaded it in August 2014, they massacred or enslaved whomever they could. Thousands of women were sold as sex slaves."[89]

A twelve-year-old victim spoke about her ordeal following her escape after 11 months of rape at the hands of her "owner": "He told me that according to Islam he is allowed to rape an unbeliever. He said that by raping me, he is drawing closer to God …He said that raping me is his prayer to God."[90]

The horror is endless. Stories continue to leak out of IS controlled areas about children who are torn rom their families and "given" to IS fighters as sex slaves, of the men who rape them many times a day, of public gang rapes, and of young girls and women who commit suicide rather than submit to the dishonor of rape.

"Their stories can be told … but you can't show her face or give her name. … Once, after a girl was interviewed, her face clearly visible, her family – still in captivity with IS – was killed."[91]

---

[87] "Sexual terror: ISIS 'fatwa' outlines when and how militants can rape female prisoners," ManipalWorldNews.com, December 29, 2015.
http://www.manipalworldnews.com/2015/12/29/sexual-terror-ISIS-fatwa-outlines-when-and-how-militants-can-rape-female-prisoners/
[88] "The Business of the Caliph" *ZietOnline* December 2014.
http://www.zeit.de/feature/islamic-state-is-caliphate
[89] "All I Can Do Is Tell Their Stories" by Rose George. *The Rotarian*, February 2016. Page 36.
[90] JihadWatch.org by Robert Spencer, October 13, 2015.
http://www.jihadwatch.org/2015/08/he-said-that-raping-me-is-his-prayer-to-god
[91] "All I Can Do Is Tell Their Stories" by Rose George. *The Rotarian*, February 2016, page 39.

The brutality of the system is not limited to the foot soldiers of IS, but goes straight to the most senior IS leaders, who have set the example of doctrinally-sanctioned savagery. Self-proclaimed IS Caliph Abu Bakr al-Baghdadi took U.S. hostage Kayla Mueller as his own, personal sex slave.

Under his "protection," she was tortured and repeatedly raped by al-Baghdadi before her death.[92] For him, according to later reports from several Yazidi girls who were enslaved with her, rape was his "reward" for IS victories.

Kayla Meuller

It is difficult for the Western mind to comprehend the mindset that allows human beings to treat others with such malice and brutality. But IS fighters, like jihadis throughout history, have no trouble justifying it with specific citations from the Qur'an, hadith, *Sira*, and shariah. Take, for example, the following paragraph that exalts kidnapping and enslavement of young Christian girls in Africa and equates it with the reward of Allah. It appeared in the English version of *Dabiq*, Issue 8:

> For years, the mujāhidīn of West Africa stood firm against the apostate and crusader forces who were attempting to wipe out any traces of Islam in the region. They stood firm in the face of slander and opposition by the evil scholars and other hypocrites. They stood firm when their leader, the mujāhid Shaykh Muhammad Yūsuf (rahimahullāh), was executed by the apostate Nigerian police. They did not fear the blame of any critics when they captured and enslaved hundreds of Christian girls, even as the crusader media machine put the brunt of its strength into focusing the world's attention on the issue. They stood firm, so Allah

---

[92] "ISIS leader Abu Bakr al-Baghdadi repeatedly raped U.S. hostage Kayla Mueller and turned Yazidi girls into personal sex slaves" by Judit Neurink. AugU.S.t 14, 2015. http://www.independent.co.uk/news/world/middle-east/ISIS-leader-abu-bakr-al-baghdadi-exposed-as-serial-rapist-of-hostages-who-made-women-his-personal-10456237.html

increased their strength, hastened their victory, granted them consolidation, and humiliated their enemies.

In the course of a U.S. Special Operations Forces raid on a Syrian target on the night of May 15, 2015, top IS financial official, Tunisian Abu Sayyaf, was killed. A large cache of documents was found at the site, documents containing operational records and religious *fatwas*, among them pamphlets that justify and codify the enslavement and rape of captive non-Muslim women (see Appendices II and III). According to the documents, girls as young as ten years old are included among those with whom IS men are permitted to have sexual relations.

When the Yazidi girls who lived in the house with Kayla Meuller escaped, they pointed to Umm Sayyaf, Abu Sayyaf's Iraqi wife, who was captured in Syria in May 2015 by U.S. Special Forces, as the organizer of the sex trafficking.[93] The captured records showed that her work was efficient. By mid-August, 2014, more than 5,000 Yazidi girls and women had been sold into sexual slavery by IS. Over 3,000 of those are still thought to be in captivity.[94]

In late 2014, IS published a pamphlet with a Q&A format, explaining the "proper" treatment of slaves (see Appendix III), all in complete accord with authoritative Islamic doctrine. To date, IS has received in excess of $28 million from ransoms collected for kidnapped victims, and untold millions more from the sex slave trade.

---

[93] Ibid.
[94] "ISIS Enshrines a Theology of Rape" by Rukmini Callimachi. *The New York Times*, Aug 13, 2015, http://www.nytimes.com/2015/08/14/world/middleeast/isis-enshrines-a-theology-of-rape.html?_r=0

PART III:
LIFE UNDER THE ISLAMIC STATE

The harshest enforcement of sharia is imposed on those living under IS control. The minimum includes mandatory prayer in a mosque five times a day and required female "modesty" for all women, which means that every woman is forced to wear the full, body-covering *chador* with a veil (*hijab*) and *niqab* which covers all of a woman's face but her eyes.

In return, IS provides the population with some social services, including health and welfare programs, bread factories, and food distributions to needy families. Unlike the Taliban, IS participates in polio-vaccination campaigns for local children. They have also established a number of religious schools for children, including schools for girls, and live-in "training camps" for "cub scouts." Another part of IS' governance is to provide for infrastructure construction and repairs.

Early on, IS established a Consumer Protection Authority that has forced shops, supermarkets, and even kebab stands to close for selling what IS inspectors consider to be poor quality or forbidden products. IS' first (and only so far) "Annual Report",[95] published in 2014, carried an interview with Abu Mohammed, head of the Consumer Protection Office, in which he said the following:

> "The Consumer Protection Office is one of the departments of the Islamic Services Committee, which is supervised by the Islamic State of Iraq and Shaam. It's an office that's concerned with protecting shoppers by inspecting the goods being sold in shops, markets, shopping centers and whole-sale outlets, discovering goods that are spoiled or not suitable for sale and taking those responsible to account. Likewise, we inspect restaurants and sweet-shops, and monitor slaughterhouses, so we can keep people from getting sick and guard against harmful substances."

---

[95] *Islamic State Report,* https://azelin.files.wordpress.com/2014/06/islamic-state-of-iraq-and-al-shc481m-22islamic-state-report-122.pdf

When asked how infractions are dealt with, he responded:

> *"If the issue of complaint is verified and we seize harmful products or products that aren't fit for consumption, we raise the issue to the Islamic legal court so it can order that the shop be closed down for a specified period, or for the owner to pay a fine. In some case, the penalty reaches the level of a prison sentence if the spoiled product has directly harmed the Muslims."*

In fact, they have burned cartons of cigarettes and bottles of alcohol (considered *haram* or "forbidden" under shariah), tortured, murdered, and crucified those they judged non-compliant, and desecrated graves and shrines, which they consider blasphemous.

IS also bans instrumental music, television, and electronic communications. According to the Middle East Research Institute (MEMRI), the population living under IS control may be asked to "volunteer" to abide by IS regulations, but if they do not, punishment may be harsh.

> *"On March 28, 2016, Al-Himma Library, an IS publishing house, released a leaflet listing 20 reasons why residents in territories under the group's control should destroy their satellite dishes. In the downloadable version of the leaflet, which was published on Al-Himma's Telegram channel and shared by pro-IS accounts on Facebook and Twitter, the group warned that those who do not comply would be punished by the religious police."[96]*

---

[96] "ISIS Gives Residents In Its Territories 20 Reasons To Destroy Their Satellite Dishes, Threatens To Punish Those Who Do Not," http://www.memrijttm.org/ISIS-gives-residents-in-its-territories-20-reasons-to-destroy-their-satellite-dishes-threatens-to-punish-those-who-do-not.html

Integral to the IS justice system is the imposition of the *Hudud* punishments, which are mandatory and may not be modified, because both the crimes and their corresponding punishments are explicitly spelled out in the Qur'an. Among these are amputation of hands and feet for theft, crucifixion, execution for apostasy, flogging for fornication, and stoning to death for adultery.[97]

LIFE IN RAQQA

The city of Raqqa is the "capital" of the Islamic State. Described earlier as "the sixth largest city in Syria, relatively prosperous, it boasts energy resources and an agricultural economy." Raqqa has been described by a resident as an unremarkable city as "a dusty place far from the country's other major cities. It offered few amenities and most Syrians I knew complained about it, if they chanced to visit. It was true that the local population, a mixture of tribes and settled Bedouins, was almost entirely Sunni Muslim, but unlike such western Syrian cities as Hama and Aleppo, it didn't have a tradition of Islamic activism. As a resident of al-Tabqa, a town near Raqqa with an air base that was captured by IS in August, put it: 'The irony is we were famous for not praying!'" [98]

Since its capture by IS, the character of the city has changed dramatically. Most non-Sunni religious structures in the city have been demolished, most notably the Shi'ite Uwais al-Qarni Mosque, which was built as a combined project by Syria and Iran and completed in 2003. It was blown up by IS in May 2014.

---

[97] For an authoritative description of the Hudud crimes and punishments, see *The Hudud* by Muhammad Ata Alsid Sidahmed, 1995. http://www.amazon.com/hudud-specific-criminal-mandatory-punishments/dp/9839303007/ref=sr_1_4?s=books&ie=UTF8&qid=1461108635&sr=1-4&keywords=hudud

[98] "How ISIS Rules" by Sarah Birke. *New York Review of Books*, February 5, 2015. http://www.nybooks.com/articles/2015/02/05/how-ISIS-rules/

Shi'ite Uwais al-Qarni Mosque in Raqqa

Uwais al-Qarni Mosque after IS destroyed it

As IS' presence became felt in every aspect of life in Raqqa, fear became the prevailing emotion of the citizens. A group of activists calling themselves "Raqqa is Being Slaughtered Silently" has been posting videos showing the harsh reality that life in Raqqa has become. The group, an effort by citizen journalists devoted to exposing human rights abuses by IS, has been called an "enemy of Islam" by IS, and the activists do their work at enormous personal risk. Freedom of the press (a thoroughly Western concept) does not exist under IS because there is no such thing in Islam. In a video produced by the *Wall Street Journal*, a man who uses the pseudonym "Abu Ibrahim," says that since IS took over Raqqa, the city is run like a "police state." One young man who fled the city after IS came, told reporter Ruth Sherlock that IS had cut the city's Internet and phone lines, and shooting video or taking photos had become a crime punishable by death.[99]

Crime and Punishment, IS-Style

In the 14th issue of *Dabiq,* issued on April 13, 2016, IS set forth a clear distinction between its followers, whom it considers *real* Muslims, and those who do not follow Islam's rigid ideology:

> *Contrary to popular misconception, riddah (apostasy) does not exclusively mean to go from calling oneself a Muslim to calling oneself a Jew, Christian, Hindu, Buddhist or otherwise. In reality, there are only two religions. There is the religion of Allah, which is Islam, and then the religion of anything else, which is kufr.*[100]

On October 30, 2015, RBSS reported the deaths of an anti-IS activist and his friend whom he found beheaded in Turkey. "One of our member called 'Ibrahim' and another friend called 'Fares' were found slaughtered in their house in Urfa," a statement on Twitter said.[101]

---

[99] "Raqqa: Fear and treachery inside Islamic State's capital" by Ruth Sherlock reporting from Gazientep, Turkey. *The Telegraph,* June 15, 2015.
http://www.telegraph.co.uk/news/worldnews/islamic-state/11674734/Fear-and-treachery-inside-Isils-capital.html

[100] "Kill the Imams of Kufr in the West" *Dabiq* Issue #14, April 13, 2016, page 8.
file:///U.S.ers/hollisarmstrong/Desktop/Monographs/ISIS/Dabiq%2014%204-13-16.pdf

[101] "ISIS beheads 'Raqqa is Being Slaughtered Silently' activist and friend in Turkey" by Lizzie Deardon. *The Independent,* October 30 2015.
http://www.independent.co.uk/news/world/middle-east/ISIS-beheads-raqqa-is-being-slaughtered-silently-activist-and-friend-in-turkey-a6714911.html

Another activist, who calls himself "Abu Mohammed" said IS has undercover informers and brutal enforcers who patrol the streets looking for people who have broken the rigid IS laws. He reported the IS' first execution of a female journalist, Ruqia Hassan, who reported on life in Raqqa as it really was. Her final tweets were "I'm in Raqqa and I received death threats, and when IS

FACEBOOK

Citizen journalist Ruqia Hassan

[arrests] me and kills me it's ok because they will cut my head and I have dignity it's better than I live in humiliation with IS [sic]."[102]

Al-Aan, a satellite television station based in Dubai Media City, United Arab Emirates, reported that Hassan's family was informed of her execution on charges of "espionage" by IS on January 2, 2016.[103] To understand such charges, it is necessary to realize that Islam is as least as much — if not more — a political system as a "religion." To violate the laws of Islam is therefore not merely a "sin" or moral infringement, as in the Judeo-Christian sense of the term, but more to the point, a political act of treason.

The activists say that IS imposes strict curfews on the residents of Raqqa. Access to water is unreliable, and residents are forced to use public fountains and wells for their household water supply. The average cost of food has tripled under IS and has left residents subsisting on bread, hummus, and falafel. Cigarettes and alcohol are banned, and public burnings of the contraband are frequently seen in the streets of the city.[104]

---

[102] "Ruqia Hassan: ISIS executes first female citizen journalist in Raqqa, confirmed by 'Raqqa is Being Slaughtered Silently'" by Kate Ng. *The Telegraph,* January 5, 2016.
http://www.independent.co.uk/news/world/middle-east/ruqia-hassan-ISIS-executes-first-female-citizen-journalist-in-raqqa-confirmed-by-raqqa-is-being-a6797036.html
[103] Ibid.
[104] "Life Inside the ISIS Home Base of Raqqa, Syria" *Wall Street Journal* video. YouTube. September 15, 2014.
https://www.youtube.com/watch?v=C14Yu0nJCVg&ebc=ANyPxKr6cxTcd3Sbo6SMspscBqgN

"The first crucifixion came early that spring—a horrific event to recall even now. Everyone at the table remembered the shock of it. Then came more: two people, shot in the head by IS executioners, crucified, and left for days for all to witness in the city's main traffic roundabout."[105]

The people in Raqqa (and, one assumes, elsewhere in the places which IS controls) are afraid to speak against IS, even in their homes. According to "Abu Ibrahim," IS offers money to boys as young as 16 to tell them who is speaking against them.[106]

One of the most egregious punishments against children was the reported killing of a seven-year-old boy "after they heard him cursing divinity while playing in the street with his friends." The boy was shot in the city of Raqqa in front of his sobbing parents. According to the report, the boy was sentenced to death by an Islamic court because "the act was considered an insult to the Caliphate, regardless of the age of the boy."[107]

Nevertheless, reports keep coming out of Syria showing a renewed courage on the part of Syrian civilians, who risk their lives every day in order to get their stories out. Women are secretly filming gruesome executions, landmark buildings that have been destroyed and left in rubble, and armed IS guards patrolling the city streets, now deserted by residents who fear the IS supporters who rule their city.[108] One video shows how IS has turned the Armenian Catholic Church of the Martyrs in Raqqa into police headquarters.

Other reports include the crucifixions, beheadings, live mass burials of men, women, and children, burning men alive by suspending them on spits over a fire, and the taking of women and girls as sex slaves. Not satisfied to brutalize the general population, they have also turned on their own. When,

b8v57YVqUM8TUVMAPLAnSWrdikHuEpm3WlAZnREGGKsvay4ixAVt7AOD8JOoQ9DLqRB OGQ

[105] "Telling the Truth About ISIS and Raqqa" by David Remnick. *The New Yorker,* November 22, 2015. http://www.newyorker.com/news/news-desk/telling-the-truth-about-ISIS-and-raqqa

[106] "Life Inside the ISIS Home Base of Raqqa, Syria," YouTube video.

[107] ISIS reportedly executes 7-year-old boy for cursing while playing with friends," FoxNews.com, May 9, 2016. http://www.foxnews.com/world/2016/05/09/isis-reportedly-executes-7-year-old-boy-for-cursing-while-playing-with-friends.html?intcmp=latestnews

[108] "'They execute with bullets, decapitate the body, stick the head on a spike and put it on display at the roundabout': Syrian women risk execution as they use hidden camera to film life in Raqqa under ISIS" by Julian Robinson. MailOnline.com, March 14, 2016; updated April 11, 2016. http://www.dailymail.co.uk/news/article-3491190/They-execute-bullets-decapitate-body-stick-head-spike-display-roundabout-Syrian-women-risk-execution-U.S.e-hidden-camera-film-life-Raqqa-ISIS.html

in January 2016, IS soldiers lost the city of Ramadi to the Iraqi army, they fled to Mosul, where IS gathered them in the city square and burned them alive as a warning to other IS fighters.

IS AND WMD

Throughout its campaign to conquer Iraq and Syria, there have been persistent reports regarding IS' repeated use of chemical weapons against the civilian populations, as well as against the Kurds in northern Iraq. In February 2016, U.S. forces captured the head of the IS division that was set up as the R&D unit for the development of chemical weapons.[109]

The man, identified as Sleiman Daoud al-Afari, has reportedly been revealing important details about the program since his capture, although the use of chemical weapons by IS has continued. On March 12, 2016, *The Guardian* reported[110] that IS had launched a pair of chemical attacks near the Iraqi city of Kirkuk, killing a three-year old girl and wounding 600 others.

On April 5, *Syrian State TV* reported that IS had used mustard gas against Syrian soldiers in an attack on a military airport in Deir al-Zor.[111] The wounded in these attacks suffered from burns, severe breathing difficulties, and dehydration. The chemicals used by IS attacks up to this point were identified as low-grade mustard gas and chlorine.[112]

IS FORGIVES NO ONE

In January 2016, a 14-year-old boy was declared an apostate by IS for missing Friday prayers in the town of Jarablus, Syria, and was decapitated in a public execution that his parents were forced to attend.[113] Similarly, on March 5,

---

[109] "U.S. Captured Top ISIS Chemical Arms Engineer," Associated Press, as reported by ABC News, March 9, 2016. http://abc7.com/news/iraqi-officials-U.S.-captured-top-ISIS-chemical-arms-engineer/1238015/

[110] "ISIS Launches Two Chemical Attacks in Northern Iraq" Associated Press, March 12, 2016. http://www.theguardian.com/world/2016/mar/12/ISIS-launches-two-chemical-attacks-in-northern-iraq

[111] "Islamic State militants use mustard gas in attack on Syrian troops: Syrian State TV" as reported by *i24News*, April 5, 2016. http://www.i24news.tv/en/news/international/middle-east/108599-160405-islamic-state-militants-U.S.e-mU.S.tard-gas-in-attack-on-syrian-troops-syrian-state-tv

[112] Ibid.

[113] "14-year-old Syrian Boy Misses Friday Prayers Then ISIS Does This" by Yochanan Visser February 2, 2016. http://www.westernjournalism.com/14-year-old-syrian-boy-misses-friday-prayers-then-ISIS-does-this/

2016, a sixteen-year-old boy in the same town was arrested by IS' secret police services, also on the charge of heresy, for missing Friday prayers. He, too, was publicly beheaded.[114] On February 19 in the city of Mosul, a 15-year old boy was publicly beheaded outside the main mosque for listening to American popular music on a portable CD player in his father's store.[115]

Teenager executed for missing Friday prayers

As time passes, there is no cessation in the brutality that IS brings to the cities over which it rules. On April 10, a man was publicly beheaded and his headless body crucified in Raqqa after having been convicted in a Shariah court for apostasy and "fighting the Caliphate." The verdict was read court by a man wearing a black mask:

> *"We hereby behead this apostate according to the Caliphate's rules. We hang his dirty corpse to be an example for those who dare to fight alongside the Caliphate's enemies."*[116]

---

[114] "Boy, 16, beheaded by ISIS after failing to appear for Friday prayers" by Maayan Groisman, *Jerusalem Post,* March 223, 2016   http://www.jpost.com/Middle-East/Boy-16-beheaded-by-ISIS-after-failing-to-appear-for-Friday-prayers-447050

[115] "ISIS extremists publicly behead Iraqi teenager for 'listening to western music'" by Ahmed Shiwesh. http://aranews.net/2016/02/ISIS-extremists-behead-iraqi-teenager-for-listening-to-western-music/

[116] "ISIS executes, crucifies Syrian man on charges of 'fighting the Caliphate,' " April 11, 2016. http://aranews.net/2016/04/ISIS-executes-crucifies-syrian-man-charges-fighting-caliphate/

IS has lived up to its reputation for brutality in every place it has conquered. A UN "Report on the Protection of Civilians in the Armed Conflict in Iraq: 1 May – 31 October 2015"[117] spares no detail in the litany of crimes against the people of Iraq during this brief period. The cruelty with which the murder of former elected officials, former candidates, and other civilians in the Mosul region were murdered between June 23 and July 10, 2015, is made no less chilling by the crisp, impersonal way in which it was described in this UN report:

> *"On 23 June, ISIL posted a video showing the killing of 16 men. The video, of seven minutes duration, showed the killing of the men in three batches – by a rocket-propelled grenade fired at a car in which some men were placed, by placing others in a cage that was submerged into water, and by decapitating the remainder with explosives. The men were allegedly accused of cooperating with ISF. The men, dressed in red jumpsuits, are shown allegedly confessing in parts of the video.*

> *"On the evening of 3 July, ISIL killed the former local Mayor (Mukhtar) of Ain Marmiya village, Makhmour district, south-east of Mosul, Ninewa. The victim, who was shot in the head, had been abducted by ISIL from his house on 21 June, accused of cooperating with the Peshmerga and ISF.*

> *"On 10 July, after Jum'a (afternoon) prayers, nine people were killed by ISIL in the Bab al Tob area of central Mosul, Ninewa. The victims were forced to lie down on the street and a bulldozer was driven over them. The victims reportedly included at least one former ISF officer. The killings occurred in front of a large crowd and were intended as a warning to the population."*

Through the acquisition of massive wealth, the judicious use of its treasury, and its obsession with keeping track of all the various aspects of its operations, IS significantly expanded its clout wherever it was able to expand. They acquired resources, weapons, territory, and influence. Combined with their ruthlessness, they were able to command most of the areas they set out to conquer, acquiring dominance over much of northern

---

[117] "Report on the Protection of Civilians in the Armed Conflict in Iraq: 1 May – 31 October 2015" by the United Nations Assistance Mission for Iraq (UNAMI) and the Office of the United Nations High Commissioner for Human Rights (OHCHR).
http://www.ohchr.org/Documents/Countries/IQ/UNAMIReport1May31October2015.pdf

Syria and also much of northern Iraq. Most recently they have begun inspiring and sponsoring attacks beyond the Middle East, most notably in the November attacks in Paris, as well as attacks in Turkey, California, the downing of a Russian airliner over the Sinai desert, and the coordinated attacks in Brussels.

IS has shown itself to be technologically competent, as well as brutal and ruthless. The possession of so much lethal material in their hands portends dire situations for those who fail to submit to the will of Islam.

PROLIFERATION

IS' forays into Syria laid the groundwork for rapid growth. Its ruthless style of conquest through rape, torture, and murder have made them feared and hated, enabling IS to gain power through fear, to build its war chest, and to set its sights beyond Iraq and Syria.

In mid-2014, IS appeared unexpectedly in Gaza and in the Sinai. On June 29, mourners at a funeral in Gaza were observed carrying the black and white flags of IS for one of the two terrorists, whose body was also draped in an IS flag. The two terrorists had been targeted in an Israeli airstrike for firing rockets from Gaza into populated areas of Israel. It was the first time that public signs of support for IS had been seen in Gaza, which is strictly controlled by HAMAS, another Sunni Islamic terrorist group. Because it is customary for the body of a "martyr" to be buried in the flag of his organization, the fact that the terrorist's body was wrapped in the IS flag would suggest a more than casual affiliation with the group.

The Egyptian Army claimed that fifteen IS operatives had infiltrated the Sinai over the weekend of June 28, 2014, but were captured, and that other IS fighters had been entering the Sinai from Gaza via tunnels. HAMAS flatly denied these allegations because it demonstrated its lack of control in the areas they are supposed to govern. Infiltration of Sinai, however, which had become a terrorist playground after its return by Israel to Egypt, was a logical place where IS could seek to expand into additional territory.

Those early reports were confirmed in November 2015, when IS brought down a Russian commercial airliner with a bomb placed on it at the Sharm el Sheikh Airport. The plane went down with 224 people on board in the middle of the Sinai desert with no survivors. In its 12th edition of *Dabiq*, its glossy e-magazine, IS wrote of this attack:

"Shortly after the Russian airstrikes began, the resolute soldiers of the blessed Shāmī Wilāyah of Saynaʾ succeeded in downing a Russian passenger plane, resulting in the deaths of 224 Eastern crusaders. The operation exacted revenge upon the cross-worshippers for recently killing hundreds of Muslims in Shām, including their women and children. And the Islamic State will continue to strike Russia until Shariʿah returns to all the lands of the Muslims usurped by the crusader Russians and until Russia pays the jizyah in humiliation."[118]

Today IS-affiliated groups are firmly ensconced in the Sinai, where Egypt has been contending with HAMAS and other terrorists for years. Sinai's rugged mountainous terrain and wide empty plains provide terrorists with highly effective cover and operating space. In particular, *Wilayat Sinai*, the IS-affiliated group that took credit for bringing down the civilian Russian airliner over Sinai in 2015, has been the target of Egypt's campaign called "Operation Right of the Martyr 2." In January 2016, Egypt carried out a bombing raid against *Wilayat Sinai*, in which they claimed to have killed 60 IS militants. Nevertheless, Sinai continues to be a hotbed of activity for IS-affiliated groups who train there, attack Egyptian military, police, and civilians, and who pose a serious threat to Israel, its neighbor to the north.[119]

As IS expands its territory, it is determined to destroy all the artificial national boundaries created in the Arab/Muslim world by the 1916 Sykes-Picot Agreement.[120] The agreement established British and French spheres of influence in the Middle East after the defeat of the Ottoman Empire in WWI and established artificial boundaries between the states which these borders created. More broadly, this was the attempted export of the Westphalian nation state system to a region that, aside from a very few places like Egypt, had never been organized in this way before then. Clans, tribes, ethnic and sectarian groups had always vied for conquest and dominance, extending

[118] "You Think They are Together but Their Hearts Are Divided," *Dabiq* Issue 12, page 43. December 2015. https://azelin.files.wordpress.com/2015/11/the-islamic-state-e2809cdc481biq-magazine-12e280b3.pdf

[119] "ISIS Receives a Blow in Sinai as Egypt Attacks Terror Stronghold with Airstrikes" by Abra Forman. *Breaking Israel News,* January 3, 2016. http://www.breakingisraelnews.com/57848/egyptian-airstrikes-kill-up-to-60-ISIS-militants-in-northern-sinai-middle-east/#qfAIg6UIkD8VtDzv.97

[120] "Iraq ISIS Crisis: Is This the End of Sykes-Picot?" by Gianluca Mezzofiore. *International Business Times,* June 30, 2014. http://www.ibtimes.co.uk/iraq-ISIS-crisis-this-end-sykes-picot-1454751

the borders of caliphates and empires as far as they could go—but the concept of discrete, fixed, often artificial boundaries for a self-contained, sovereign 'country' simply did not—and in many places still does not—exist. And because that concept never really caught on across vast expanses of the Middle East and North Africa (MENA) region, in the post-colonial period, things are coming apart now.

In particular, Islamic forces seek to destroy whatever is left of the Westphalian system in the MENA region and beyond in order to fulfill the prime directive of Islam: conquest and subjugation of the entire world under a single Islamic government, called a Caliphate (or Imamate for Shi'ites) under rule of Islamic Law (shariah). Today's Islamic State renewed the process of erasing nation state borders that has been pursued off and on via jihad since the 7th century. Taking out the borders among the former Iraq and Syria and their neighbors, in order to re-establish an Islamic Caliphate to rule over a united Sunni territorial base, is only the first step of IS' ultimate plan that remains true to Muhammad's original vision of 14 centuries ago.

The driving aims of IS were clearly demonstrated as they first took control of vast areas of land in the former Syria and Iraq and invigorated its recruitment program. Elsewhere, too, IS sought to establish a presence: in Libya, where the government has failed and much of the country is in chaos, the reported number of IS fighters rose from 200 in 2014 to 2,000 in 2015,[121] and kept rising until, by the beginning of 2016, the figure approached as many as 6,000.[122] This is, in part, attributed to the fact that it is now easier for foreign fighters to get into Libya than into Syria, and because the chaos in north-eastern Libya is conducive to the movement of IS jihadis. In Qaddafi's hometown of Sirte, IS has made itself at home. In fact, IS now controls an area of approximately 200 km around the city. This give IS access to the Europe just across the Mediterranean and provides a path to all of Africa.

According to Jonathan Spyer, "Sirte is no dusty backwater. It has an extensive infrastructure, including a seaport, and an international airport. It is also adjacent to two sites vital to the oil industry on which Libya relies –

---

[121] "ISIS Spreading in Africa?" by Aaron Morrison. December 1, 2015.
http://www.ibtimes.com/ISIS-spreading-africa-islamic-state-fighters-grew-thoU.S.ands-east-west-regions-2206851

[122] Size of ISIS force declining in Iraq and Syria, according to new intel" by Andrew Tilghman, *Military Times,* February 4, 2016.
http://www.militarytimes.com/story/military/2016/02/04/new-intel-shows-ISIS-force-declining-iraq-syria/79819744/

the Sidr oil port and the refinery at Ras Lanuff."[123] The opportunity for IS in Libya is only just beginning to make itself apparent.

Through the sworn allegiance of Boko Haram in Nigeria, which was reported to have been responsible for 6,644 deaths in 2014 alone,[124] and the newly-created IS affiliate, Jabha East Africa (an off-shoot of al-Shabaab),[125] IS has begun to enlarge its Caliphate into countries throughout the African continent.

Wherever IS goes, it brings the savage ideology of jihad and shariah with it. In February 2015, IS demonstrated its presence in Libya, releasing a video in which they paraded twenty-one Coptic Christians along a Libyan beach and beheaded them, with the final frames showing their blood flowing into the Mediterranean and mixing with its waters.[126]

IS ASPIRATIONS

In December 2015, the Arabic newspaper *Asharq al Awsat* reported that IS terrorists in Sirte, Libya, were training on an imported flight simulator designed for commercial airlines.[127] According to the article, a senior Libyan officer said that a group of IS leaders, including retired officers from Libya and a number of neighboring countries, obtained the simulator in October. A second simulator, this one designed for fighter jets, was also reported to have arrived in Sirte as well. The types of simulators being used are still unknown.

The Libyan Air Force was reported to have made several attempts to hit at least one of the bases where the training is thought to be taking place, but the

---

[123] "Black Banner at the Gates of Europe" by Jonathan Spyer. The Rubin Center. April 30, 2016. http://www.rubincenter.org/2016/04/black-banner-at-the-gates-of-europe/?utm_source=activetrail&utm_medium=email&utm_campaign=Rubin%20Newsletter,%20May%205,%202016

[124] "ISIS overtaken by Boko Haram as world's deadliest terror organization", by Rase Troup Buchanan. *The Independent*, November 17, 2015. http://www.independent.co.uk/news/world/africa/boko-haram-overtakes-ISIS-as-worlds-deadliest-terror-organisation-a6737761.html

[125] "ISIS: New terrorist group Jabha East Africa pledges allegiance to 'Islamic State' in Somalia" by Lizzie Deardon. *The Independent*, April 8, 2016. http://www.independent.co.uk/news/world/africa/ISIS-new-terrorist-group-jahba-east-africa-pledges-allegiance-to-islamic-state-in-somalia-a6974476.html

[126] "ISIS claim of beheading Egyptian Copts in Libya shows group's spread" by Ian Black, *The Guardian*, February 15, 2015   http://www.theguardian.com/world/2015/feb/15/ISIS-21-egyptian-coptic-christians-beheading-libya

[127] "ISIS in Libya Train to Fly Planes" by Abdul Sattar Hatita. *Asharq al-Awsat*, December 2, 2015. http://english.aawsat.com/2015/12/article55345705/ISIS-in-libya-train-to-fly-planes

operations were unsuccessful, in part because the Libyan Air Force is said to lack sufficient weapons to ensure success in such raids. In a return to the Libyan theater (albeit this time, unlike in 2011, opposing the jihadis), two U.S. Air Force F-15s carried out a strike on an IS training camp in northern Libya on 19 February 2016, reportedly hitting a safe house and killing 41 people. A local official said the dead were "probably members" of IS.[128]

One successful strike will not end the war, however, and IS continues to expand its operations in Libya with only limited opposition from the West. Driven by an ideology based on 7th-century doctrine that has been fixed by the scholars of Islam since the 10th century, neither IS nor the overall global forces of Islamic jihad are likely to give up on the commandment of the faith to build a global Caliphate. Rather, having begun to acquire territory and populations under its control, IS' next mission is to continue to increase the number of its followers around the world massively, primarily by attracting the allegiance of pre-existing Islamic terror groups, Muslim populations, and individual jihadis.

---

[128] "'ISIL training camp' in Libya targeted by U.S." Al-Jazeera, February 20, 2016. http://www.aljazeera.com/news/2016/02/deaths-reported-raids-isil-camp-libya-160219131122223.html

Part IV   65

PART IV:
HOW THE ISLAMIC STATE GROWS

The explosive growth of IS has not been accidental. IS has applied a variety of strategic and tactical methods to achieve its dramatic growth systematically and rapidly. From its initial use of partners to help fulfill initial goals, to the inventive and resourceful use of technology, IS' mission has been, from the beginning, to seize and hold the land and populations that will be the foundation of its caliphate.

STRATEGIC PARTNERING

When IS first burst on the scene in Iraq in 2014, it demonstrated an alarming show of power, taking much of the world by surprise, by rapidly expanding its power in a number of ways. The first was through the establishment of strategic alliances to achieve the conquest of Iranian puppet regimes in the former Iraq and Syria. Despite its failed attempt to merge with Jabhat al-Nusra in 2013, IS' strategic plan for growth continued to rely on attracting the allegiance of other jihadist organizations.

One of its earliest strategies to generate growth and attain power was to create alliances with other groups. IS forged alliances with some 41 different groups as it moved its forces from northern ccept changes

Syria into Iraq and southward towards Baghdad. There they recruited many of the men who were formerly in Saddam Hussein's military, but who had been marginalized after the U.S. entered Iraq.[129]

In addition to alliances with smaller groups like the Islamic Army, a Sunni rebel faction, IS teamed up with the Army of the Men of the Naqshbandi Order (a major Sunni spiritual order of Sufis). While the Naqshbandi Order traces its lineage back to the earliest days of Islam, this group emerged in late 2006, led by former members of Saddam Hussein's Ba'ath party.

---

[129] Following America's invasion of Iraq in 2003, a de-Baathification program was instituted in which more than 400,000 Sunni members of the defeated Iraqi Armed Forces (IAF) were relieved of duty and were barred from further employment by the Iraqi government. Some of those soldiers and officers who had been dismissed but were allowed to keep their weapons, formed local insurgent forces, and later joined the emerging al-Qa'eda in Iraq militants, which later became IS. (Source: http://www.ocnus.net/artman2/publish/Analyses_12/The-Role-of-Iraqi-Former-Regime-Elements-in-Islamic-State_printer.shtml)

Commanded by Izzat Ibrahim al-Duri, Saddam's former deputy, the Naqshbandi still enjoy considerable popularity in Iraq. At the time IS began its rampage through Iraq, the Naqshbandi were reported to include the loyalty of thousands of soldiers, including many who had been members of the Iraqi army under Saddam Hussein, before the U.S. invasion. Although their leaders seemed to have a great deal of influence over IS, the relationship was more expedient than ideological, and in the end, the Naqshbandi not only added considerable military experience to the IS army, but also filled many leadership positions in the emerging IS organization, including Intelligence, . In fact, of IS's 23 government ministries, Naqshbandi officers head three of the most crucial: security, military and finance.[130]

In addition to the alliances it made, IS also recruited tens of thousands of fighters from across the entire world, including the West, to join their fight, first in Syria and Iraq, and more recently in Europe and the U.S. In April 2016, a new terrorist group calling itself Jabba East Africa broke off from the al-Qa'eda-in-the-Arabian-Peninsula (AQAP)-affiliated al-Shabaab in Somalia and pledged bayat (allegiance) to the Islamic State. In their statement, they said:

> *"We in Jabha East Africa are advising all East Africans to leave al-Shabaab and their sponsor groups, like al-Muhajiroun, al-Hijra and Ansar Islam. ... Like al-Shabaab the sponsor groups have not understood the binding obligation of the Khalifah (caliphate).*
>
> *"We are telling the mujahideen in East Africa that al-Shabaab has now become a psychological and physical prison.*
>
> *"To pledge bayah to Caliph Abu Bakr al-Baghdadi is freedom for the mujahideen in East Africa and opportunity to wage jihad according to the Sunnah against the enemies of Allah."*[131]

---

[130] "How Saddam's men help Islamic State rule" by Isabel Coles and Ned Parker. Reuters.com, December 11, 2015.

[131] "Islamic State Expands to East Africa With New Allegiance Pledge" The Clarion Project, April 10, 2016. https://www.clarionproject.org/news/islamic-state-expands-east-africa-new-allegiance-pledge

RECRUITMENT

In February 2015, Director of the National Counterterrorism Center Nicholas Rasmussen told Congress that some 20,000 foreign fighters from 90 countries had traveled to Syria to join the fighting there; 3,400 of those fighters were thought to have come from Western nations. Among them, a total of 250 Americans have traveled or attempted to travel to Syria as of September 2015, although only about 150 have been successful, according to FBI Director James Comey.[132]

In the four years since its first appearance in the Syrian conflict, IS has surged in size and strength, in both the former Syria and Iraq. In fact, between 2014 and the beginning of 2015, the number of foreign fighters who joined IS increased from 12,000 to 27,000. By 2016, this number had reached 36,000, a direct result of the highly sophisticated recruitment practices employed by IS.

One of the consequences of this groundswell of support was that IS now had the battle-trained manpower to begin targeting the *kuffar* beyond the Middle East, especially as so many countries inexplicably continued to allow fighters who'd been to Middle East battlefields to return home. By mid-2015, IS claimed to have its own fighters in countries throughout Europe and the United States, as well as in Libya, Egypt, Sinai, and Gaza. In 2014, the CIA estimated that IS had between 20,000 and 31,500 fighters. More recent estimates put the number at closer to 100,000. How many of those IS fighters and ideological supporters may be present inside U.S. territory remains an open question.

FATAL ATTRACTION: THE MAGNET OF IS

> *"IS, the Islamic State in Iraq and Syria, is using every contemporary mode of messaging to recruit fighters, intimidate enemies and promote its claim to have established a caliphate, a unified Muslim state run according to a strict interpretation [sic] of Islamic law. If its bigotry and beheadings seem to come from a distant century, its use of media is up to the moment."*[133]

---

[132] "ISIS: Trail of Terror" by Lee Ferran and Rym Momtaz. ABCNews.com http://abcnews.go.com/WN/fullpage/isis-trail-terror-isis-threat-U.S.-25053190

[133] "ISIS Displaying a Deft Command of Varied Media" by Scott Shane and Ben Hubbard. *The New York Times*, Aug. 30, 2014. http://www.nytimes.com/2014/08/31/world/middleeast/isis-displaying-a-deft-command-of-varied-media.html?_r=0

Since the rise of IS in Syria and Iraq, and its spread to countries in many other parts of the world, it is estimated that over 4,000 Westerners have left their homes to join the ranks of IS, including some 550 women.[134]

A question that looms large in any discussion of the Islamic State is why thousands are drawn to a group that is so openly savage, that promotes itself through violent videos of the murders it commits, and offers promises of the afterlife to would-be jihadis who travel half-way around to world to join it. Although the reality of Muslims' devotion to their faith and the sacrifices it demands of them are explained incessantly by IS in online websites, pronouncements and publications, speeches, and videos, it remains difficult for Westerners, especially the current Western leadership that is so woefully ill-educated about Islam and its doctrine, few analysts, national security figures, or reporters seem able to grasp the simplicity or fervor of true belief.

Instead, a range of theories, often based on nothing more substantive than psychobabble, proliferate. One theory offered in a book review that appeared in the July 24, 2015 issue of Atlantic Magazine suggests, "The recent migrations to IS, just like the political pilgrimages before them, are yet further testimony to the power of wishful thinking and how desire can trump reason."[135] The author, Simon Cottee, writes about IS, "It promises, in short, salvation and ultimate meaning through total commitment to a sacred cause." To support his thesis, he quotes sociologist Karl Mannheim, who wrote, "Wishful thinking has always figured in human affairs. When the imagination finds no satisfaction in existing reality, it seeks refuge in wishfully constructed places and periods."[136]

Instead of studying the source of IS' compelling lure in the Islamic doctrine, law, and scriptures that define it, analysts too often prefer to indulge in theories about yearning for a more utopian society that does away with the inequities and failures of the one people live in, imagining that Muslims are simply engaging in wishful thinking, accepting IS' call to jihad in order to achieve relief from their current existence, or allowing their "wishful

---

[134] "ISIS In America: From Retweets To Raqqa" The Program on Extremism, Center for Cyber and Homeland Security (CCHS) at George Washington University.
https://cchs.gwu.edu/sites/cchs.gwu.edu/files/downloads/ISIS%20in%20America%20-%20Full%20Report.pdf

[135] "Pilgrims to the Islamic State" by Simon Cottee. *The Atlantic,* July 24, 2015.
http://www.theatlantic.com/international/archive/2015/07/ISIS-foreign-fighters-political-pilgrims/399209/

[136] Ibid.

thinking" to subvert their critical thinking. Generally speaking, this is simply not realistic but the stories abound, nevertheless.

Mirsad Omerovic, 34, who is known by the Islamic name of "Ebu Tejma," was a recruiter who traveled around Europe "like a pop star on tour," and even had his own YouTube channel, according to the prosecutor who tried his case. Omerovic aimed his message at young Muslims aged between 14 and the late twenties.

Samra Kesinovic and Sabina Selimovic

Samra Kesinovic, 17, and Sabina Selimovic, 16, were among those who are portrayed as being swept up in the rhetoric and the "pop star" reputation of Omerovic, who offered "to carry out brainwashing" on those who viewed his videos. Omerovic is believed to have been the man who recruited the two girls known as IS' "Poster girls." The two were daughters of Bosnian immigrants who fled their country in the 1990s during the war in the former Yugoslavia and settled in Vienna, Austria. They were reportedly enticed to join IS and traveled together to Syria, where they were married to IS fighters. In 2015, reports came from Syria that Samra wanted to return home and had been beaten to death when she tried to escape from Raqqa, and Sabina was thought to have died in the fighting there.[137]

---

[137] "ISIS teen 'poster girl' Samra Kesinovic 'beaten to death' as she tried to flee the group" by Alexander Sehmer. *The Independent,* November 25, 2015.

Omeric was arrested in November 2014 in his home, which was, according to the prosecutor, "stuffed with jewelry, cash and savings books worth a fortune when it was stormed by Austria's elite heavily-armed police special forces team."[138]

INTERNET RECRUITING - SOCIAL MEDIA

One of IS' sharpest tools for recruitment has been the extensive and resourceful use of social media, which it employs universally to promote its successes through messaging and video.

In its effort to spread its message, grow its ranks, and raise money, IS has mastered an area that jihadis have been working on for years but never managed to conquer – the successful use of the Internet for propaganda and recruitment.

IS recruiters, supporters, and fighters use a wide range of social media, including Facebook, Twitter, Ask.fm, Pinterest, YouTube, WordPress, Kik, WhatsApp, and Tumblr to communicate with each other and to recruit new jihadis. The numbers of would-be warriors has grown exponentially.

In its 2014 "annual report," IS stated its goal:

> "Spreading Islamic knowledge, correcting the people's understanding of the religion, and clarifying the truth are all from among the most important goals of the Islamic State of Iraq and Shaam [Greater Syria]."

The use of the Internet to recruit new jihadis to its cause was not original, but it served as a vehicle to exploit 21st century technology with enhanced imagination and energy. The resources upon which some of its methods are based are similar to the guidelines used by al-Qa'eda, some of which are found in "A Course in the Art of Recruiting,"[139] which began appearing on jihadi websites in 2009. IS republished it in 2015 as a dumbed-down

---

http://www.independent.co.uk/news/world/europe/ISIS-teenage-poster-girl-samra-kesinovic-beaten-to-death-by-group-as-she-tried-to-flee-killings-a6747801.html

[138] "Islamic State recruiter traveled through Europe 'like a popstar on tour'" by Robert Spencer. February 22 2016. http://www.jihadwatch.org/2016/02/islamic-state-recruiter-traveled-through-europe-like-a-popstar-on-tour

[139] "A Course in the Art of Recruiting" Compiled by Abu Amr Al Qa'idi, Translated by Abu Mujahid and Abu Khalil
https://ia800300.U.S..archive.org/32/items/ACourseInTheArtOfRecruiting-RevisedJuly2010/A_Course_in_the_Art_of_Recruiting_-_Revised_July2010.pdf

document, intended for the less-educated but shariah-savvy jihadi recruiters to help them through the process of bringing others into the IS fold.

Dr. John Horgan, forensic psychologist and analyst of terrorist behavior at Georgia State University in Atlanta, Georgia, agrees that IS recruiters have become extremely savvy social media users. "Recruitment is an intensely personal experience," he said. "IS is so good at it because [they] recognize the tailor-made efforts with teenagers. They'll use North American young 20-somethings to target teenagers, [or] they'll use females to target female teenagers, [or] they'll use English speakers to target English speakers."[140]

What al-Qa'eda was able to do with only limited success, IS has done by exploiting the magic of social media as a force multiplier in order to recruit tens of thousands. Through the use of media like Twitter and YouTube, IS idealizes the process of joining the group on behalf of Islam, sometimes promising "humanitarian work" (for the girls) and "fighting for Islam" (for the boys). Many are convinced that they are joining for a noble cause, while others join for the power and blood lust, and others for a quest for the "romance" of warriors and war. Once there, however, most of the girls become "wives" for jihadi fighters and are subjected to a life of rape and humiliation. All too often, they are murdered.[141] The males are thrown into the heat of battle for which they are often similarly unprepared.[142]

There are many theories, of course, about why young Westerners leave the relative security of life in Europe and the U.S. and opt to join IS in the Syrian war zone. Many seem desperate to grasp at any explanation except the obvious one: belief in Islam and commitment to fighting *fi sabilallah* (in the way of Allah). Some theories posit a need to be a part of something more powerful when one feels un-empowered, or the appeal to one's basest instincts when rage and unfulfilled expectations make the primitive brutality in IS' actions a compelling siren call. The idea of having power (over enslaved women, for example) can be enticing, they would have us believe, when one feels powerless, and the thought of achieving paradise as a hero, and being greeted by 72 virgins for an eternity of sexual bliss is no doubt

---

[140] "This Is How ISIS Uses Social Media to Recruit American Teens" by Dorian Geiger. *Teen Vogue,* November 20, 2015.

[141] ISIS 'Pin-Up Girls' - Before and After" Clarion Project, December 2, 2015.
http://www.clarionproject.org/news/ISIS-pin-girls-and-after

[142] "This is How ISIS U.S.es Social Media to Recruit American Teens" by Dorian Geiger. *Teen Vogue,* November 20, 2015 http://www.teenvogue.com/story/ISIS-recruits-american-teens

tantalizing. All these are offered up as among the reasons why young Western men might seek to join IS.

For those unfamiliar with the Islamic faith, it is less clear why young women want to give up their lives in the West and opt for a life in purdah as an IS wife. IS' carefully crafted high-tech message on social media paints a glowing picture of life for pious Muslim women under IS.

> *"While their husbands are out fighting, these women communicate IS's message to the outside world, and particularly to other women curious about the same cause. Because of their youth and Western upbringings, they do so in slang and emoji, intermixed with a handful of Islamic phrases that they have picked up. As the recent widespread distribution of beheading videos on U.S. social media has shown, IS brings plenty of propaganda savvy to its brutal campaign."*

"Maria" from a Skype capture

In a March 14, 2016, article, [143] an American woman who calls herself "Maria" and uses the title of "media coordinator" was reported to be using the Internet to recruit schoolgirls from Northern Ireland to join IS. Using encrypted messaging apps, which are popular among IS recruiters because they make tracking their activities difficult, Maria also uses "Emojis" and text-speech because they appeal to the teenage audience she is targeting.

She doesn't talk to potential recruits about the horrors that face jihadi wives, but rather of the mission. "We don't bring people here because it is a fantasy, they come here because they have a cause and a purpose to serve," she tells them.[144] That cause and that purpose are the advancement of Islam on earth.

This American-born IS recruiter may earn as much as $10,000 for each recruit she delivers to IS. From her perspective, IS represents the future, and she

---

[143] "U.S. jihadi woman lures Northern Ireland schoolgirls to join ISIS" *Belfast Telegraph,* March 14, 2016. http://www.belfasttelegraph.co.uk/sunday-life/U.S.-woman-attempts-to-lure-northern-ireland-schoolgirls-into-joining-ISIS-34537328.html
[144] Ibid.

seems confident that 2016 will be one to remember for the Islamic State, as she says, "a year of success and achievements."[145]

For some, the indoctrination is complete. At the age of 17, Hoda Muthanas, a Yemeni-American woman from Hoover, Alabama, began to immerse herself in Islamic literature that she found online. She created a new identity on Twitter and gained thousands of followers, which allowed her to interact with like-minded Muslims around the world.

Saying she was going to Atlanta, Georgia, for a college field trip, she went instead to the airport and got on a flight to Turkey. From Turkey, she went to Syria, where she married a foreign fighter from Australia, who later died in an airstrike. She continued to work the Internet with her Tweets, using an account @ZumarulJannah. On one occasion, she uploaded a picture of four Western passports, with the caption, *"Bonfire soon, no need for these anymore."*

Using her account @ZumarulJannah (now suspended), "Umm Jihad" expressed her deep contempt for the United States. "Soooo many Aussies and Brits here," she tweeted. "But where are the Americans, wake up u

---

[145] Ibid.

cowards." If other American IS supporters couldn't make it to Syria, she said, "Terrorize the kuffar [non-Muslims] at home." [146]

On March 19 she tweeted, "Americans wake up! … Men and women altogether. You have much to do while you live under our greatest enemy, enough of your sleeping! Go on drive-bys and spill all of their blood, or rent a big truck and drive all over them. Veterans, Patriot, Memorial etc Day parades..go on drive by's + spill all of their blood or rent a big truck n drive all over them. Kill them." [147]

Hoda is reported to still be in Syria, where she continues to be an active recruiter for IS on Twitter. For others, like Samra and Sabina, the end of the story is tragic. The realities of life under IS are brutal. If you are not among the powerful, you are likely to be a victim.

RECRUITMENT THROUGH VIDEOS

As-Sahab was al-Qa'eda's in-house propaganda factory, producing "documentary-quality films, iPod files, and cellphone videos." [148] The quality was, at the time, considered to be outstanding, although by today's standards, their clips were relatively primitive. Still, no terrorist organization had ever used this kind of technology to promote itself in such a sophisticated way. Their videos were usually professionally-taped speeches and scenes of al-Qa'eda leaders, with their weapons at their side or in the background.

In the early years following 9/11, distribution of the videos was cumbersome. Initially, delivery was made by *as-Sahab* at a physical dead-drop every few days. It was only in 2005 that they began using the Internet to deliver them. *As-Shahab* sent them to press outlets, which might or might not air all or portions of them.

It was the first time that an enemy had invested in a professional studio to present to the world their vision and their plans to destroy us. The purpose of the videos was to make statements to the world and remind the West in

---

[146] "Gone Girl: An Interview With An American In ISIS" by Ellie Hall. BuzzFeed.com http://www.buzzfeed.com/ellievhall/gone-girl-an-interview-with-an-american-in-ISIS#.py00KnQ8y

[147] Ibid.

[148] "Al-Qa'eda's Growing Online Offensive" by Craig Whitlock, Washington Post Foreign Service. Washington Post, June 24, 2008. http://www.washingtonpost.com/wp-dyn/content/article/2008/06/23/AR2008062302135.html

particular that al-Qa'eda was a force to be reckoned with. The videos were generally formal, with Osama bin Laden or another senior al-Qa'eda official sitting in front of a camera with a weapon beside him and the symbols of al-Qa'eda around him. He would speak to the camera, presenting his current message to the world.

IS also creates its own videos, using its in-house company *al-Hayat*, and its videos are often graphic and deeply disturbing, containing violent acts of murder. IS then posts them to millions of viewers on social media. The difference is staggering.

IS revealed its interest in using video to spread its message with the graphic video-taped beheading of American journalist James Wright Foley by "Jihadi John."[149] When IS first aired this video and broadcast its anti-U.S. message, the world viewed it in horror. Over the course of time, the videos became increasingly professional, with multiple cameras, multiple takes, and special effects.

IS has placed a high priority on exploiting advanced technology to push its message out. The *Al-Hayat* Media Center calls itself the "The Media Wing of IS" and is the provider of IS videos and web content. Frustrated by successful efforts to shut down its websites for jihadis, *al-Hayat* has now created a new hub on the darknet, in order to thwart most efforts to shut them down. On the day after the Paris attacks, for example, *al-Hayat* launched its first propaganda website on the dark Web, initiating it on a new dark hub with a new video celebrating the coordinated terrorist attacks.[150]

As in other areas of IS endeavors, the use of videos was taken to another level from where al-Qa'eda left off, while authorities and activists continue to try to shut down its online infrastructure.

---

[149] "Jihadi John" was a British citizen who joined IS and became known for his role in brutally beheading IS victims with a knife. He was killed in a drone strike on November 12, 2015 as he left a building in Raqqa.

[150] "ISIS Moves To The Dark Web To Spread Its Message And Avoid Detection by David Gilbert. *International Business Times,* November 19, 2016. http://www.ibtimes.com/ISIS-moves-dark-web-spread-its-message-avoid-detection-2191593

ENGLISH LANGUAGE RECRUITMENT

In the summer of 2010, al-Qa'eda in the Arabian Peninsula (AQAP) produced its first Internet magazine, *Inspire*, which it promoted online. The goal of this glossy e-magazine was to recruit English speaking, wannabe *jihadis* to join al-Qa'eda's war against the West. The magazine included how-to articles that taught its readers how to, for example, "Make a bomb in the kitchen of your mom" (Issue 1), and how to use a car as a WMD, as well as first-person accounts and encouragement for individual jihad (as in Issue 9).

They also include articles like "I am proud to be a traitor to America" by American jihadist and editor of *Inspire* Samir Khan (Issue 2), [151] weapons training (Issue 8), "Torching Parked Vehicles" and "Causing Road Accidents" (Issue 10), and "Car Bombs Inside America" (Issue 12).[152] In short, *Inspire* is more about tactics than strategy, more about operations than the supremacy of Islam, and it justifies terrorism politically rather than theologically.

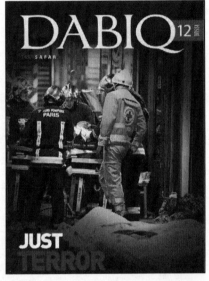

Dabiq. In 2014, IS took a leaf out of al-Qa'eda's book and published its first issue of *Dabiq*, a similar type of glossy Internet magazine. But IS took the concept much further than al-Qa'eda, as both a tool for recruitment and a reinforcing statement about Islam. *Dabiq* is named after a town in northern Syria, a key site in Muslim eschatology where they believe the final battles of "Armageddon" between the forces of Islam and the West will occur.

Shaykh Abu Mus'ab az-Al-Zarqawi (rahimahullah) anticipated the expansion of the blessed jihad from Iraq into Sham and linked it to this hadith saying,

---

[151] Khan was later killed with Anwar al-Awlaki in a U.S. airstrike in Yemen on 30 September 2011.

[152] Links to all issues published to date can be found at https://ds-drupal.haverford.edu/aqsi/resources/jihadi-magazines?sort_by=title&sort_order=DESC

"The spark has been lit here in Iraq, and its heat will continue to intensify – by Allah's permission – until it burns the crusader armies in Dabiq"

[Ayna Ahlul-Muru'at] [153]

Published in multiple languages, the magazine aims to provide encouragement and guidance in the recruitment of new jihadis throughout the West. But unlike *Inspire, Dabiq* takes the message much further, and stays close to the concept of spreading the Islamic message. Unlike *Inspire*, it does not put the Gregorian date on the cover, and it focuses on what IS considers to be a higher plane, while bringing the realities of its barbarism to the fore. Colin Clarke, a political scientist at Rand, says, "Dabiq is a far more comprehensive attempt to recruit westerners than Inspire. It's really a one-stop shop for all things IS."[154]

The title of an August 2014 New Republic article by Josh Kovensky says it all: "IS's New Mag Looks Like a New York Glossy—With Pictures of Mutilated Bodies."[155]

Where *Inspire* featured "how to" articles on bomb-making and interviews with prominent al-Qa'eda personalities, *Dabiq* has been devoted to IS' larger, religious, military, and political messaging about Islam and the Caliphate. Its message is to the world of jihadis and wannabe jihadis and it is very clear. To the future warriors in the army of IS, the word is "obey."

It is obligatory on you, my noble brother, to harshly denounce anyone who disobeys the leader, and to assist your leader and your brothers in preventing any disobedience and mistake that the Ummah and the mujahidin would pay the price for.[156]

In its magazine, as in life, IS pulls out all the stops – nothing is too brutal, incendiary or violent to find its way onto the pages of *Dabiq*. It stands a

[153] See issue, #12 at http://www.clarionproject.org/docs/islamic-state-isis-isil-dabiq-magazine-issue-12-jU.S.t-terror.pdf

[154] "IS's New Mag Looks Like a New York Glossy—With Pictures of Mutilated Bodies" by Josh Kovensky. *The New Republic.* AugU.S.t 25, 2014. https://newrepublic.com/article/119203/ISs-dabiq-vs-al-Qa'edas-inspire-comparing-two-extremist-magazines

[155] Ibid.

[156] "Advice to the Mujahadin: Listen and Obey" by Isa Ibn Sa'd al Ushan. *Dabiq*, Issue #12, page 9.

reflection of the single-minded purpose of IS, to support the core commandment of Islam: to conquer and subjugate the earth to shariah.

RECRUITMENT OF CHILDREN - IMPRESSMENT

In 2002, the United Nations Children Fund (UNICEF) defined child soldiers as "any child—boy or girl—under eighteen years of age, who is part of any

kind of regular or irregular armed force or armed group in any capacity."[157] But the impressment of far younger children into armies of the world, particularly in the Middle East and Africa, is a phenomenon that has a long history. Today, it is esti-mated that there are 300,000 children

RE FEATURES

Iranian boys on their way to the Iran-Iraq War circa 1980s

fighting in 30 different conflicts around the world. Among the most notable examples of child soldiers in the twentieth century were the Hitler *Jugend* (Hitler Youth) and Iran's military use of boys as young as twelve, who were sent to the front during the Iraq-Iran war in the 1980s to serve in mine field clearing and as human waves against fortified Iraqi positions.[158]

HAMAS uses children to help build their tunnels from Gaza into Israel. In 2012, *The Journal of Palestine Studies*[159] reported that 160 children had died building HAMAS' notorious tunnels,[160] first used to smuggle drugs,

---

[157] "Child Soldiers Around the World" by Eben Kaplan. Council on Foreign Relations, December 2, 2005 http://www.cfr.org/human-rights/child-soldiers-around-world/p9331
[158] "Iranian boys head to the front" November 21, 2013.
https://www.reddit.com/r/HistoryPorn/comments/1r5mh3/iranian_child_soldiers_head_to_the_front_during/
[159] "Gaza's Tunnel Phenomenon: The Unintended Dynamics of Israel's Siege," Institute for Palestine Studies. http://www.palestine-studies.org/journals.aspx?id=11424&jid=1&href=fulltext
[160] Ibid.

weapons and commercial goods into Gaza, then later expanded to infiltrate Israeli territory to carry out terror attacks.[161]

HAMAS has also set up special programs, camps, and schools to train their young boys to be fighters and killers in the war against Israel. And HAMAS is far from alone. According to Human Rights Watch, "Thousands of children are serving as soldiers in armed conflicts around the world. These boys and girls, some as young as 8 years old, serve in government forces and armed opposition groups. They may fight on the front lines, participate in suicide missions, and act as spies, messengers, or lookouts. Girls may be forced into sexual slavery. Many are abducted or recruited by force, while others join out of desperation, believing that armed groups offer their best chance for survival." [162]

But IS has taken this to a new low. IS takes young boys from their families and hardens them to fight. They are drilled in warfare and trained to fight. One of their methods entails forcing the young boys they capture to fight each other in steel cages.

On June 21, 2015, an article[163] appeared in the British *Daily Mail*[164] about how IS forces boys as young as six to fight each other while an adult beats them with a stick (see photo, below). One seven-minute propaganda video, released on social media, shows shockingly young boys wrestling inside a giant ring, and crawling through metal tubes as IS fighters fire live rounds over their heads. "IS has become infamous for recruiting youngsters – or "cubs of the caliphate" – by instructing them in the Islamic doctrine of the *Shaheed* (or "martyrs," as they call them) when they die on the battlefield or in suicide attacks."[165]

---

[161] "Child Labor Deaths in HAMAS Tunnels Are No Surprise" by Spencer Case. *National Review*, July 24, 2014. http://www.nationalreview.com/article/384004/child-labor-deaths-HAMAS-tunnels-are-no-surprise-spencer-case

[162] Child Soldiers" ww.hrw.org/topic/childrens-rights/child-soldiers

[163] "ISIS trains young boys by forcing them to CAGE fight" http://www.express.co.uk/news/world/586122/Video-ISIS-train-young-boys-forcing-cage-fight

[164] ISIS' Cage of Death" by Jay Akbar. *Daily Mail*, June 21, 2015. http://www.dailymail.co.uk/news/article-3133238/ISIS-cage-death-Terror-group-forces-young-boys-wrestle-inside-giant-steel-ring-beats-sticks-train-generation-killers.shtml

[165] "ISIS trains young boys by forcing them to CAGE fight"

In late 2015, IS posted a video showing child soldiers being forced to "play" a bloody game of hide and seek. In the video, they are sent up a hill to search for, find, and kill a prisoner inside an ancient castle in a remote part of eastern Syria. The prisoners, who are accused of spying for al-Assad, and are described as "sons of Jews," are sent with their hands bound, into various parts of the castle to wait for the children. One by one, each of the boys, some of whom are as young as eight, is given a pistol with live fire. Each boy is told to find a prisoner and execute him at close range. When one boy returns, he gives his pistol to the next boy.[166] The video also shows the boys studying the Qur'an, and learning about close combat and self-defense.

> *"The children who managed to escape describe how they were indoctrinated into the jihadi group's radical brand of Islam [sic] and taught that they should execute their "unbeliever" [infidel] parents. ... "We weren't allowed to cry but I would think about my mother, think about her worrying about me and I'd try and cry quietly," he [an escapee] said. ... Some children who managed to escape IS and are now living in the refugee camps in northern Iraq, have also been left badly psychologically scarred. The repeated beatings and endless propaganda have meant that some of the*

[166] "A chilling case for war: ISIS CHILD soldiers in Syria", by Tom Wyke. *Daily Mail Online*, December 4, 2015. http://www.dailymail.co.uk/news/article-3344897/ISIS-child-soldiers-play-horrifying-Hide-seek-game-search-ruins-prisoners-shoot-head-latest-shocking-footage.html#ixzz3znDSpesT

escapees wake up in the night with nightmares while others suffer seizures."[167]

The report goes on to say, "The growing trend for IS to use child soldiers as suicide bombers, particularly in Iraq, has been suggested as a sign of how stretched their resources are in the region." [168]

The latest figures of IS' use of child soldiers were published by the Combatting Terrorism Center (CTC) at West Point, and the numbers are shocking:

"From January 1, 2015, to January 31, 2016, 89 children and youth were eulogized in Islamic State propaganda. Fifty-one percent were alleged to have died in Iraq, while 36 percent died in Syria. The remainder were killed during operations in Yemen, Libya, and Nigeria. Sixty percent of the sample was categorized as "Adolescent" based on Islamic State photographs, 34 percent were classified as "Older Adolescent," and 6 percent were "Pre-Adolescent." Thirty-one percent were Syrian, 25 percent Syrian/Iraqi, and 11 percent Iraqi. The remaining 33 percent were from Yemen, Saudi Arabia, Tunisia, Libya, the United Kingdom, France, Australia, and Nigeria.

"Of the 89 cases, 39 percent died upon detonating a vehicle-borne improvised explosive device (VBIED) against their target. Thirty-three percent were killed as foot soldiers in unspecified battlefield operations, 6 percent died while working as propagandists embedded within units/brigades, and 4 percent committed suicide in mass casualty attacks against civilians. The final 18 percent were inghimasi (derived from the Arabic "to plunge"), meaning they died in what we more commonly term marauding operations in which a group of mostly adult fighters infiltrates and attacks an enemy position using light automatic weapons before killing themselves by detonating suicide belts. Forty percent of the time, the children and youth died in operations targeting state security forces (including military and police targets). Twenty-one percent

---

[167] "Raymond Ibrahim: Why the Islamic State's Ancient Jihadi Tactics 'Shock' the West" by Raymond Ibrahim. February 26, 2016 http://www.jihadwatch.org/2016/02/raymond-ibrahim-why-the-islamic-states-ancient-jihadi-tactics-shock-the-west

[168] Ibid.

were killed fighting against paramilitary forces (militias and non-state opposition), and only 3 percent carried out suicide attacks against civilians. No target was specified for the remaining 36 percent."[169]

The use of children as combatants is illegal under international law. Rule 136 of the 1949 Geneva Convention IV states: "States Parties shall refrain from recruiting any person who has not attained the age of fifteen years into their armed forces. ... Under Article 8(2)(b)(xxvi) and (e)(vii) of the 1998 ICC Statute, "conscripting or enlisting children under the age of fifteen years" into armed forces or groups constitutes a war crime in both international and non-international armed conflicts." [170]

As mentioned earlier, however, IS does not abide by the Geneva Conventions but follows only Islamic Law (shariah).

EXPLOITING THE SYRIAN REFUGEE CRISIS

Abdullāh Ibn 'Amr (radiyallāhu 'anhumā) said that Allah's Messenger (sallallāhu 'alayhi wa sallam) said, "There will be hijrah after hijrah. The best people on earth will be those who keep to the land of Ibrāhīm's hijrah. Then there will remain on the earth the worst of its people. Their lands will cast them out, Allah will hate them, and the fire will gather them together with the apes and swine."

*[Hasan – Reported by Imām Ahmad,
Abū Dāwūd, and al-Hākim]*[171]

As a result of the barbarous treatment of indigenous populations in the regions IS conquers, the flow of refugees from the now-broken Iraq and Syria has overwhelmed other countries. First Turkey and Jordan, and then countries throughout Europe have been inundated by over a million refugees, far beyond what they can absorb. The 2015-16 tsunami of refugees,

---

[169] "Depictions Of Children and Youth in The Islamic State's Martyrdom Propaganda, 2015-2016" by Mia Bloom, John Horgan, Charlie Winter. *CTC Sentinel*, February 18, 2016. https://www.ctc.U.S.ma.edu/posts/depictions-of-children-and-youth-in-the-islamic-states-martyrdom-propaganda-2015-2016

[170] "Practice Relating to Rule 136. Recruitment of Child Soldiers" IRC Customary IHL https://www.icrc.org/cU.S.tomary-ihl/eng/docs/v2_rul_rule136

[171] *Dabiq* Issue #3, back cover.

ostensibly from Syria, flooded Europe and threatened to engulf the world as increasing demands were made on Western countries to take them in.

IS has taken full advantage of the crisis. Even in the early days of the human deluge, analysts suggested that only 20% of those coming into Europe were actually Syrians.[172] And the vast majority of "refugees" were young, single men from places like Afghanistan and Albania. IS uses this flood of humanity to infiltrate its fighters into Europe on stolen or forged passports. Early on, IS claimed that it had already sent "thousands" to infiltrate the flow of refugees in order to pursue its jihad against the West, a statement that has already been proven tragically true.

An IS fighter who has found a new career smuggling "refugees" into Europe, told BuzzFeed[173] in September 2015 that the ongoing clandestine operation has been a "complete success. … Just wait," he smiled. "It's our dream that there should be a caliphate not only in Syria but in all the world and we will have it soon, God willing. … They are going like refugees," he explained. "Others just go to Europe to be ready."[174]

He told BuzzFeed that IS has more than 4,000 "ready" fighters throughout the European Union, which makes this less of a refugee problem about those fleeing the fighting in Syria, and more a dangerous *hijra* or migration[175], which is a religious duty for Muslims who participate in civilization jihad and enables them to spread the rule of Islam throughout the world.

Historically, there have been two major examples of *hijra*. The first was the Islamic expansion from what is today the Arabian Peninsula outwards to the

---

[172] "Four out of five migrants are NOT from Syria: EU figures expose the 'lie' that the majority of refugees are fleeing war zone" by Ian Drury for *The Daily Mail*, September 15, 2015.
http://www.dailymail.co.uk/news/article-3240010/Number-refugees-arriving-Europe-soars-85-year-just-one-five-war-torn-Syria.html#ixzz3tJSTB9oD

[173] BuzzFeed.com

[174] "ISIS smuggler: 'We will Use refugee crisis to infiltrate West" by Leo Hohmann. *World Net Daily*. September 4, 2015. http://www.wnd.com/2015/09/ISIS-smuggler-we-will-U.S.e-refugee-crisis-to-infiltrate-west/

[175] *Hijra* means "migration" in Arabic, but its meaning carries much more significance. To Muslims, the *hijra* was the event in 622 CE, when Muhammad and his small group of followers fled the city of Mecca to Yathrib, which Muhammad renamed "Medina." When he arrived there, Medina had a Jewish majority, but by the time Mohammed conquered Mecca eight years later, most of the pagan and Jewish populations had either converted to Islam, had fled, or were dead. In Muslim belief, the *hijra* therefore pertains to the movement of a group of Muslims from a predominately Muslim area to a predominately non-Muslim area, for the purpose of establishing Islam's dominance there; in other words, *jihad* by migration.

north, east and west, reaching as far as West Africa, central France and Uzbekistan from 632 to 750. The second *hijra* reached its peak when Islamic armies besieged Western Europe right up to the gates of Vienna in 1683, where they were finally stopped. When the Muslims were driven back by Polish Catholic forces into the Balkan Peninsula, the back of the Ottoman Empire was effectively broken, although the final collapse didn't come until WW I, when Constantinople/Istanbul was occupied by British, French and Italian forces until 1923. The Ottoman Caliphate, the last one before the current 21st century Caliphate, was abolished the following year by Mustafa Kemal (who became known as "Ataturk").

Today, Europe faces a new onslaught. As IS continues to spread its influence across the Middle East and North Africa, the coordinated attacks in Paris, France on Friday, November 13, 2015 represented the first major strike at the heart of Western civilization. Through these six simultaneous attacks, IS demonstrated its goal to establish itself in Europe through terror and chaos in order to seize power.

What we are witnessing in Europe and North Africa is the beginning of a great Islamic invasion, a *hijra* unlike anything the West has ever dealt with before. Additionally, IS wages war against those Muslims seen as apostates, backsliders, or simply insufficiently obedient to shariah. In this, the Islamic State models itself after the first Caliph after Muhammad, Abu Bakr, who fought the Ridda Wars in just the same way, to return by force those whom Muhammad had brought under the black flag of Islam but who then tried to break free after his death, reportedly in 632 CE. The great Islamic reformer, Ibn Wahhab, likewise formed an alliance with the House of Saud for precisely the same reasons: to bring wayward Muslims back to obedient practice of the faith. The present jihad against Christians, Yazidis, other non-Muslim minorities, as well as unfaithful Muslims, which began in Syria, has now spread to other parts of the Middle East, Northern Africa, Europe, and the United States.

In December 2015, a coalition of Western states began to mobilize and use their combined air power to take out some of IS' more obvious and viable targets – the oil infrastructure from which IS has been raising nearly 50% of its revenue. But even this step was limited, as former CIA official Michael Morell told PBS' Charlie Rose show in late November 2015, because of

Obama administration concern over possible environmental damage.[176] The U.S. military also thoughtfully dropped leaflets to warn oil tanker truck drivers of impending strikes, so they could "get away from their trucks first."[177]

In February 2016, the U.S. captured the head of the IS chemical weapons program, Sleiman Daoud al-Afari, in the town of Badoosh, northwest of Mosul. Al-Afari was an engineer in Hussein's military and joined IS early on. Based on intelligence received from al-Afari, the U.S. was able to begin finding and dismantling existing weapons factories.[178]

Nevertheless, a month later IS carried out a chemical weapons attack on the civilian population of a town near Kirkuk, Iraq. Using scientists and engineers who formerly worked in the Saddam Hussein regime developing chemical weapons and the means to deploy them, IS has conducted at least twelve such attacks in 2014[179]. The low yield mustard gas weapons produced only one death in this attack, but resulted in some 800 injured.

A TURNING POINT? IS IS LOSING GROUND?

Less than two years into what looked like IS' inexorable march on Syrian and Iraqi cities, IS began losing some of its hard fought territory in battles with Iraqi and Syrian regime forces. In the final days of 2015, following the November Paris attacks, airstrikes by the combined forces of U.S., the UK, and France, as well as the uptick in U.S. special operations targeting IS leaders, began to make a substantial difference in IS' ability to hold onto its territory, particularly in the former Syria.

Following the Paris attacks on November 13, Syrian and Iraqi forces began playing an expanding role in pushing back against IS in their respective areas, with growing support from U.S., UK, French, and Russian air support. Cities like Sinjar and Palmyra have been reclaimed and the residents who

[176] Hanchett, Dan, "Morell: 'Environmental Damage' One Reason U.S. Avoided Hitting Islamic State Oil Wells," *Breitbart*, 25 November 2015.
http://www.breitbart.com/video/2015/11/25/morell-environmental-damage-one-reason-us-avoided-hitting-islamic-state-oil-wells/

[177] Lubold, Gordon and Sam Dagher, "U.S. Airstrikes Target Islamic State Oil Assets," *Wall Street Journal*, 17 November 2015. http://www.wsj.com/articles/french-airstrikes-in-syria-may-have-missed-islamic-state-1447685772

[178] http://www.theguardian.com/world/2016/mar/09/ISIS-chemical-weapons-leader-captured-iraq-U.S.-special-forces

[179] General Jack Keene, "Futures with Maria Bartiromo." March 13, 2016. FoxNewsTV.

were able to flee the IS fighters are slowly returning to their homes. When Kurdish soldiers took back the city of Sinjar in November 2015, they found several mass graves[180] of Yazidis, whom IS murdered when they carried out what the Nazis called "*selectsia*": choosing who would live and who would die, separating the young from the old and infirm, murdering the latter and selling the former into sexual slavery.

PHOTO-AFP-GETTY IMAGES

Ruins of the Palmyra ruins, post-IS

When the city of Palmyra, known for its ancient ruins, was liberated on March 27, 2016 by the Syrian Arab Army (SAA), Hizballah, and other pro-Damascus militia groups under Russian air cover, returning antiquities experts experienced both anguish and relief. They discovered that although in their religious zeal and their desire for media attention IS had destroyed much of the ancient ruins, some were still standing or could be reconstructed.[181] It appears that IS had slowed down its wanton destruction of the ancient buildings when they realized that they were also destroying

[180] "Iraq: Yazidi mass grave discovered in Sinjar" *The Guardian,* November 15, 2015.
http://www.theguardian.com/world/2015/nov/15/iraq-yazidi-mass-grave-sinjar-kocho
[181] "Syrian Troops Said to Recapture Historic Palmyra From ISIS" by Hwaida Saad and Kareem Fahim. *The New York Times,* March 27, 2016.
shttp://www.nytimes.com/2016/03/28/world/middleeast/syria-palmyra.html?_r=0

the economy of the city, which depended on the tourism that the ancient sites brought to Palmyra for its economic survival.[182]

THE VULNERABILITY OF IS

IS has found itself most vulnerable where its financial resources are concerned. In order to continue to build its caliphate, IS must be able to fund all of its complex pieces. By hitting its revenue sources and the places where its wealth is stored, it may be possible to damage its war machine and hamper its growth.

In January 2016, a U.S. airstrike took out an IS "bank" in Mosul, Iraq in which IS stored the equivalent of $90 million in cash that was used to finance IS operations, with two, 2,000-pound bombs. A week later a second bank was hit, representing a further loss to IS of $45 million. This represented a major blow to IS' ability to pay its fighters, who reportedly took a sharp cut in pay following these attacks. It also made it necessary for IS to re-evaluate areas of its financial resources and budgeting.

Britain's decision to join France and the U.S. in targeting IS oil revenues following the Paris massacre in November 2015, changed the playing field. The Royal Air Force Tornados that targeted the oil facilities in Omar, Tanak, and Jafra in eastern Syria caused IS to lose an estimated $335 million after a sustained aerial bombardment destroyed its facility at Deir ez-Zor.[183] The air campaign against IS' oil production by the U.S., Britain, and Russia started at the end of October 2015 "and is now more effectively disrupting IS's crude oil extraction. In November 2015, production fell by 30% at al-Omar and al-Tanak, the two top producing fields and those most heavily targeted by the recent offensive."[184]

---

[182] "Scenes From Palmyra Indicate ISIS Slowed Assault on Treasures" By Kareem Fahim. *The New York Times,* March 28, 2016.
http://www.nytimes.com/2016/03/29/world/middleeast/scenes-from-palmyra-indicate-ISIS-slowed-assault-on-treasures.html?action=click&contentCollection=Middle%20East&module=RelatedCoverage&region=EndOfArticle&pgtype=article

[183] "ISIS crippled with two-thirds of oil revenue wiped out as RAF jets bomb oilfields in Syria" by Tom Batchelor. *The Express,* December 3, 2015.
http://www.express.co.uk/news/world/623607/Islamic-State-jihadi-group-loses-two-thirds-oil-revenue-U.S.-airstrikes-Syria

[184] "Inside ISIS Inc.: The journey of a barrel of oil" by Erika Solomon, Robin Kwong and Steven Bernard. Updated December 11, 2015. http://ig.ft.com/sites/2015/ISIS-oil/

Between November 2015 and March 2016, it is estimated that 40% of IS-held territory has been taken back by Syrian and Iraqi forces, supported by the Western coalition air strikes. The ongoing effect of the loss of revenues from the destroyed wells, fields, the oil delivery chain, and the banks has yet to be assessed, but there is no doubt that IS must now recalculate its financial position to factor in these losses.

The series of defeats suffered by IS in both Syria and Iraq during 2015 also included the loss of key cities over which the terrorist group had taken control, such as Palmyra in Syria and Ramadi in Iraq. These losses have taken a heavy toll, not only in territory, but also in the significant number of IS fighters who died in the conflict. On the Turkish border and in north-eastern Syria, Kurdish fighters have retaken areas captured by IS and established a firm presence there, although the fighting continued to rage around them. By early 2016, the Syrian army was ramping up for an offensive to re-take the key city of Aleppo, and on April 11, 2016, the Syrian and Russian governments jointly announced the beginning of a large military operation. The aim was to encircle the remaining rebel-held districts inside Aleppo, Syria's largest city, in order to recapture and finally liberate it from IS control.[185]

In March 2016, the Iraqi army, which had already taken over Ramadi, began preparing for a subsequent invasion of the city of Mosul. Meanwhile, IS continued to maintain a defensive strategy to protect the core areas of its regime in both Mosul and Raqqa, even as other areas under its control continued to shrink.

In addition to inflicting territorial losses upon it, the coalition fighting IS continued to successfully target its senior command. U.S. aerial strikes succeeded in killing several key IS leaders, including IS's finance minister, Abu Alaa al-Afari, who was also considered second-in-command after Abu Bakr.

METASTASIZING INTO EUROPE AND BEYOND

As mentioned earlier, the flood of refugees and migrants from the Middle East into Europe has had a deadly impact on European culture, including such basic things as the safety of citizens on the streets of their own cities.

---

[185] "SAA ready to encircle Aleppo city as ISIS & rebels fight in the north by Chris Thomson." Almasdarnews.com, April 11, 2016. https://www.almasdarnews.com/article/saa-ready-encircle-aleppo-city-ISIS-rebels-fight-north-map-update/

The rate of crime and sexual assaults against Europeans has risen dramatically in only a few short months. Hidden among the legitimate refugees fleeing war in Syria are jihadis from countries throughout the Middle East.

According to European Union statistics, of 213,000 arrivals logged in April, May, and June 2015, only 44,000 of them were fleeing the Syrian civil war.[186] In April 2016, the United Nations Human Rights Commission reported that between January 2015 and April 24 2016 1,196,751 refugees and migrants entered Europe from 10 of the top refugee producing countries: Syria, Afghanistan, Iraq, Pakistan, Iran, Nigeria, Cote d'Ivoire, Guinea, Gambia, and Senegal.[187]

---

[186] Four out of five migrants are NOT from Syria: EU figures expose the 'lie' that the majority of refugees are fleeing war zone
http://www.dailymail.co.uk/news/article-3240010/Number-refugees-arriving-Europe-soars-85-year-just-one-five-war-torn-Syria.html#ixzz46yNjmVUi
[187] Refugees, Migrants Energency Response. UNHRC, April 26, 2016.
http://data.unhcr.org/mediterranean/regional.php

PART V:

THE THREAT THE ISLAMIC STATE POSES
TO AMERICA

On December 2, 2015, Sayed Rizan Farook and his wife, Tashfeen
Malik, dropped their baby off at his mother's house, and drove to
Sayed's place of work, the nonprofit Inland Regional Center in San
Bernardino, California, where a holiday party was in progress. The two were
dressed in tactical gear, and carried both handguns and illegally modified
rifles. According to a report by *The New York Times*,[188] they were armed with
four guns: a Smith & Wesson M&P assault rifle, a DPMS Panther Arms
assault rifle, a Smith & Wesson handgun, and a Llama handgun.

By the time they left the party, they had murdered fourteen of Sayed's co-
workers and wounded twenty-one others. They fled the scene, but within
hours, they too were dead, killed in a shoot-out with police. Their military-
style action was clearly well-planned and, judging from all the fire-power
and pipe bombs still in their car, this was not going to be the end of their
assault on America.

Moments before the attack, Tashfeen Malik posted a message on Facebook in
which she pledged allegiance to IS. Within minutes of the news of the attack,
Twitter was alive with messages from IS supporters, who created the
hashtags of "They are still alive and #America_burning."[189] Following the
attack, IS posted a message on Twitter, praising the couple as martyrs, and
referring to them as "two supporters of the Islamic State."[190]

While IS did not take credit for the attack, it was happy to embrace the killers
as its own and to warn America that this was only the beginning. According

---

[188] "How They Got Their Guns" by Larry Buchanan, Josh Keller, Richard A. Oppel Jr. and Daniel
Victor. *The New York Times*, December 3, 2015.
http://www.nytimes.com/interactive/2015/10/03/U.S./how-mass-shooters-got-their-
guns.html
[189] "ISIS Celebrates Killings With Twitter Hashtag" by Todd Beamon. *Newsmax*, December 2,
2015. http://www.newsmax.com/Headline/ISIS-celebrates-san-bernardino-
shootings/2015/12/02/id/704343/
[190] "ISIS Credits Itself on Twitter for San Bernardino Massacre, Threatens More" by John
Rossomando. *IPT News*, December 4, 2015. http://www.investigativeproject.org/5083/ISIS-
credits-itself-on-twitter-for-san-bernardino

to Investigative Report,[191] "A mid-level IS commander, who variously refers to himself as Jazrawi_DAESH … [wrote] 'Expect more you *kuffar* terrorists.' "

For America, although it is not likely that the Islamic State actually had anything to do with the planning and execution of the San Bernardino attack, the perception of threat from IS became real that day. But it was a relatively small-scale attack, in a small office building rather than in a large mall or theater. Americans soon forgot.

Nevertheless, the story did not end there, and indeed has not ended yet. On April 28, 2016, the Los Angeles Times reported that Federal agents had arrested the older brother of San Bernardino gunman Syed Rizwan Farook, on charges of marriage fraud, conspiracy, and lying to federal investigators.

Police also arrested his wife, Tatiana Farook, and her sister Mariya Chernykh, who were charged in a five-count indictment filed in federal court. They were accused of being involved in arranging a fraudulent marriage between Chernykh and Enrique Marquez. Marquez had already been charged with aiding in the deadly attack at the Inland Regional Center on December 2nd.[192]

But although IS was not directly involved with the attack in San Bernardino, it nevertheless played an important role as part of the network of influence that motivated Farook and Tashfeen. The constant flow of propaganda and recruiting videos and social media messages encouraging young Americans to join IS are designed to inspire and convince young Muslims to leave their lives in the West and join their brothers and sisters in IS.

Less than three months after the attack in San Bernardino, in early March 2016, IS released a video in which it pledged to the United States: *"We will kill, slaughter and burn your people. Inshallah, we will attack you very soon."* In the video, which is in English, the narrator warns President Obama that America can expect the same kind of attacks as IS carried out in Paris. The video ends with a particularly grisly and graphic beheading, in which the murderer stops in the middle, stares at the camera, then calmly continues the beheading.

---

[191] Ibid.

[192] "FBI arrests brother of San Bernardino jihad murderer and 2 others" by Robert Spencer, JihadWatch.org, April 28, 2016. https://www.jihadwatch.org/2016/04/fbi-arrests-brother-of-san-bernardino-jihad-murderer-and-2-others

IS set its sights on America long before this attack in San Bernardino. Although this was not an IS-directed attack, Malik's gratuitous online posting signaled that at least IS' inspirational reach in the U.S. was more than just words.

In 2015, American authorities arrested nearly sixty people in the United States for attempting to assist IS in one way or another, according to a new study conducted by researchers at George Washington University.[193] The study found that the vast majority of those arrested were either American citizens or permanent residents, perhaps 'home-grown', but obviously part of the Global Islamic Movement in word and deed.

Although the emergence of violent IS activity in the U.S. lags far behind that in Europe, North Africa, and the Middle East, the FBI has reported that approximately by the end of 2015, some 1,000 people in the U.S. were currently under observation for having suspected ties to IS. There were over 900 open investigations of possible IS recruits and sympathizers being carried out in all 50 states,[194] and more than 250 people had already been apprehended as jihadi wannabes who had traveled or attempted to travel to the Middle East to join IS.

According to the FBI report, 76 individuals were arrested for IS-related crimes since March 2014, 56 of them in 2015. 27% were involved in plots against the U.S.[195] Of those arrested, 40% were converts to Islam (as opposed to the general Muslim population, of whom only 23% are converts).[196] Such statistics are likely indicative of the zeal typical of converts to anything, but especially Islam. It is not clear yet how significant this number is, but it may assume growing importance as analysts further process the evolving phenomena of jihad in the U.S.

So far, the youngest person to be arrested in America on IS-related charges was an unidentified fifteen-year-old boy, according to U.S. Assistant Attorney General John Carlin, defendants under the age of 25 represent more

---

[193] "ISIS In America: From Retweets To Raqqa" by Lorenzo Vidino and Seamus Hughes Program on Extremism. The George Washington University. December 2015.
https://cchs.gwu.edu/sites/cchs.gwu.edu/files/downloads/ISIS%20in%20America%20-%20Full%20Report.pdf

[194] "FBI investigating ISIS suspects in all 50 states" by Jesse Byrnes. *The Hill,* February 25, 2015.
http://thehill.com/blogs/blog-briefing-room/233832-fbi-investigating-ISIS-sU.S.pects-in-all-50-states

[195] "ISIS In America: From Retweets To Raqqa" page 5.

[196] "Converts to Islam," Pew Research Center, July 21, 2007.

than 50% of the cases.[197] But the full number of young people who are under the radar, following jihadi websites and social media sites, is unknown.

RECRUITMENT IN THE UNITED STATES

On April 28, 2015, Seattle's Channel 4 News[198] reported that a high-ranking female IS recruiter with more than 8,000 followers on Twitter was a journalism student in her early 20s living in Seattle. Identified only by her Twitter handle, *@_UmmWaqqas*, (Umm is Arabic for 'mother' or 'mother of', and Waqqas means 'brave warrior'). Channel 4 reported that her real name is Rawdah Abdisalaam [199] , and that she was known as one of the most influential IS-linked women online.

PHOTO BY @_UMMQAQQAS

This photo of IS women, whom Rawdah called Umm Ubaydah, Umm Harithah, and Umm Layth, was posted on Rawdah's Twitter account (now closed).

Channel 4 reported that Abdisalaam was tasked by IS to deliver the message about the religious duty for Muslims to join the Caliphate, but the role she played was much more personal. She was in direct contact with British and American would-be jihadis on the eve of their departures, and she was reportedly close to a number of fighters and jihadi brides in Syria.

According to the Channel 4 report, "she's one of the final people that would-be jihadis might speak to before crossing the border to join the Islamic State group in Syria. She has been credited with considerable online and offline influence."

---

[197] "ISIS In America: From Retweets To Raqqa" page 7.

[198] "Female ISIS Recruiter is a Journalism Student Living in Seattle" by John S. Roberts. Young Conservatives, May 3, 2015. http://www.youngcons.com/female-ISIS-recruiter-college-student/

[199] "Senior female ISIS agent unmasked and traced to Seattle"
http://www.channel4.com/news/female-ISIS-women-girl-umm-waqqas-unmasked-seattle

"Flick through the group's new online "travel guidebook" and her contact details are listed, alongside 17 other agents and middlemen. Recruits are told to get in touch with these people when they make it to Turkey and want a contact in IS to help them cross the border."[200]

While encouraging mass immigration to the IS front in Syria, she herself enjoyed the creature comforts of life in the U.S. After she was exposed, the Twitter account @_UmmWaqqas was suspended. Friends say she has moved away and that her current location is unknown.

The impact of such a person, young and charismatic, should not be underestimated, and the fact that she has been doing this from within the U.S. should serve as a warning that IS supporters are already well-entrenched here and working hard to recruit Americans.

Why Are American Teenagers Attracted to IS?

There are many answers, some of them surprising. It is most commonly hypothesized that IS attracts disaffected teens who are struggling with the challenges of their age group, giving them a chance to join others in a mission that gives them purpose and a sense of belonging. IS recruiters prey on their feelings of loneliness, using social media to reach out to them. By emphasizing the sense of belonging to a mission with others just like them. The group, they are told, will embrace them and make them feel welcome, while providing a higher purpose. Sophisticated Internet videos and messaging are the tools they use to achieve the greatest impact and recruit as many jihadis as possible for IS.

'Jihadi Cool'

But the efforts of talented and highly motivated recruiters still do not completely answer the question, "What makes IS so attractive to young men and women in America?" Aside from the obvious answer that they are Muslims who respond to the call to jihad as their religion commands, a surprising number of wannabe jihadis have responded to a message that jihad is "beautiful," or even more improbably, that IS can really be "cool."

---

[200] Ibid.

Take, for example, the Twitter user "Bint Emergent",[201] an avid supporter of IS who uses Twitter and her blog to spread its message. She posts things like:

> *"Jihadis look cool — like ninjas or video game warriors — gangstah and thuggish even — the opposition doesn't."*

> *"There aren't a lot of jihadist 'poster-girls' displayed — they all wear niqab [face veil], but sometimes it's tastefully accessorized with an AK47 or a bomb belt."*

> *"Jihadis have cool weapons. And cool nasheeds[202] ... also have "young fiery imams that fight on the battlefield," whereas Team CVE[203] "has ancient creaky dollar scholars. ..."*

By putting her ideas in terms of "we" and "they," she creates an environment in which the reader is encouraged to take sides. By always referring to "them" as the ugly "opposition," she makes it perfectly clear which side the reader should be on.

In a December 2015 New York Times article entitled "The Soft Power of Militant Jihad,"[204] Thomas Hegghammer suggested, "to understand this phenomenon, we must recognize that the world of radical Islam is not just death and destruction. It also encompasses fashion, music, poetry, dream interpretation. In short, jihadism offers its adherents a rich cultural universe in which they can immerse themselves."

According to Hegghammer,[205] "there are thousands of jihadi songs in circulation, with new tunes being added every month. Jihadis can't seem to get enough *anashid (nasheeds)*. They listen to them in their dorms and in their cars, sing them in training camps and in the trenches, and discuss them on Twitter and Facebook." The *anashid* form a framework for a "highly

---

[201] "The Challenge of Jihadi Cool" by Simon Cottee. *The Atlantic,* December 24, 2015. http://www.theatlantic.com/international/archive/2015/12/ISIS-jihadi-cool/421776/

[202] A nasheed is an Islamic chant sung a capella because strict observance of Islam prohibits the use of musical instruments.

[203] CVE stands for "Countering Violent Extremism," referring to the Obama White House campaign inspired by the Muslim Brotherhood in order to divert attention and resources from actual counterterrorism efforts, but then subsequently rejected by key Brotherhood spokesmen.

[204] "The Soft Power of Militant Jihad" by Thomas Hegghammer. *The New York Times,* December 18, 2015. http://www.nytimes.com/2015/12/20/opinion/sunday/militant-jihads-softer-side.html?_r=0

[205] Ibid.

seductive subculture"[206] which touches on fashion (a blending of Western and Middle Eastern style),[207] music (*a capella* singing or chanting), poetry, and dream interpretation, a kind of Islamic mysticism that draws in the young and suggestible.

This feel-good depiction of IS stands in stark contrast to the reality on the ground in areas under IS control. And the anashid frequently have violent messages that belie the 'beauty' of the music. On April 17, 2016, Furat Media, an official Islamic State (ISIS) media wing, released a new *nasheed*, written by a well-known German ISIS operative. Denis Cuspert, a former rapper who performed under the name Deso Dogg, is also known by his Arabic name Abu Talha al-Almani.[208] He played a prominent figure in IS, and his songs and appearances in ISIS videos have been instrumental in attracting new recruits for the organization. Al-Amani was reported by the U.S. Defense Department to have been killed in a U.S. airstrike in October 2015, although IS has posted several videos of him since then and his death was never confirmed. On April 15, 2015, MEMRI posted a new *nasheed* by al-Almani called "Enemies of Allah, We Want Your Blood, It Tastes So Wonderful."[209]

This is the second verse of the *nasheed*, translated into English:[210]

> *"Brother, do not be sad; you should understand it*
>
> *"Slaughter an infidel, if you want to go to paradise*
>
> *"Take him as a hostage; you are so close to achieving your goal*
>
> *"Slaughter for Allah [and] spill a lot of blood*
>
> *"Europe, a new battlefield, go ahead and get your reward*

---

[206] Ibid

[207] Hegghammer describes a jihadi fashion statement as "sneakers, a Middle Eastern or Pakistani gown, and a combat style jacket on top."

[208] "New Nasheed By German Jihadi Denis Cuspert 'Rise Up For Slaughter' Threatens Western Cities Including Berlin, Paris, Rome, New York." http://www.memrijttm.org/new-nasheed-by-german-jihadi-denis-cuspert-rise-up-for-slaughter-threatens-western-cities-including-berlin-paris-rome-new-york.html

[209] New ISIS Nasheed In German By Rapper Deso Dogg: 'Enemies of Allah, We Want Your Blood, It Tastes So Wonderful' MEMRI.org.

[210] "New Nasheed By German Jihadi Denis Cuspert 'Rise Up For Slaughter' Threatens Western Cities Including Berlin, Paris, Rome, New York." http://www.memrijttm.org/new-nasheed-by-german-jihadi-denis-cuspert-rise-up-for-slaughter-threatens-western-cities-including-berlin-paris-rome-new-york.html

"Become martyrs over there, the virgins in paradise are already awaiting you

"Kill police officers, or apostates

"Paris, New York, and Moscow, bombs in Berlin

Chorus

"Brothers, rise up for slaughter, we are slaughtering unbelievers, capture them in an ambush, this is our religion, their blood is being spilled, Paradise is so near, Hell is their earning, because they are fighting our religion."

The song released in April 2016, called "Auf Zum Schlachten" (Rise up for Slaughter), which is sung in German and Arabic, was distributed through social media channels such as archive.org, IS-related Twitter accounts, Facebook, and Telegram. The song calls upon ISIS supporters to ambush and kill non-Muslims, promising that the Caliphate will expand and soon conquer Islamic holy sites such as Mecca, Medina, and Jerusalem. The *nasheed* threatens Europe and several Western cities, among them Berlin, Paris, Rome, and New York. On October 30, 2015, the Pentagon confirmed that Cusbert was killed in a U.S. airstrike on October 16.

There is a great divide between the horror as it is seen by Western eyes and how it is translated through the eyes of those who think they can see beauty in jihad. Hegghammer writes:

"Jihadis also weep when listening to religious hymns, watching propaganda videos, discussing the plight of Sunni Muslims or talking about the afterlife. Some weep more than others, and those who do are looked up to by those who don't.

"As the West comes to terms with a new and growing threat — horrifically evident in the recent attacks in Paris, Brussels, and San Bernardino, California — we are not only confronting organizations and doctrines, but also a highly seductive subculture. This is bad news. Governments are much better equipped to take on the Slaughterer than they are He Who Weeps a Lot."[211]

[211] Ibid.

So how successful has IS' initial recruitment program in the U.S. been? According to ICSR Department of War Studies, King's College London, more than a hundred Americans were recruited by IS in 2014.[212] IS particularly targets teenagers, male and female, to fill out its ranks.

On July 18, 2015, Safya Roe Yassin, 38, of Buffalo, New York, posted on her Twitter account, "Americans aren't even smart enough to know where to cut on a neck." Attached to this Tweet was a picture of a torso and neck with a dotted line around the base of the neck with the words "cut here." Below the dotted line, written on the torso, in Arabic, was the word *kuffar*.[213]

She also allegedly made threats against government officials and members of the military, recommending that many needed to be beheaded. The FBI had been following Yassin since January 2015, following a complaint from a "friend" on Facebook that she was using her Facebook page to try to rally support for IS. In February, 2016, FBI agents arrested her and charged her with communicating threats of violence over the Internet. Investigators said Yassin had posted the names, cities, and phone numbers of two FBI agents on Twitter in August 2015, with the words "Wanted to Kill."

Finally, there is the potent message from IS that pulls in the disaffected, the disappointed, and the disempowered. It is also reaches out to the intelligent, the sensitive, and the impressionable. A case in point is Abdirizak Mohamed Warsame, a 21-year-old Somali American who came to America as a toddler, and whom Clarion Project's Meira Svirsky describes as having "everything going for him – except the will to resist a powerful and angry narrative that eventually pulled him in."[214] His mother has been an activist, supposedly working within the Somali American community in Minnesota to prevent the so-called "radicalization" of their children (who were being raised Muslim, in shariah-adherent homes, and attending shariah-adherent mosques). As a teenager, Warsame distinguished himself as a poet, active in music and art, and he spoke out against violence.

---

[212] "Foreign fighter total in Syria/Iraq now exceeds 20,000" By Peter R. Neumann, ICSR Director, The International Center for the Study of Radicalisation and Political Violence. January 26, 2015. http://icsr.info/2015/01/foreign-fighter-total-syriairaq-now-exceeds-20000-surpasses-afghanistan-conflict-1980s/

[213] "ISIL Comes to Buffalo" BuffaloReflex.com February 24, 2016. http://buffaloreflex.com/news/isil-comes-to-buffalo/article_c7f1755e-da8d-11e5-9299-d7a4026cb011.html

[214] "From Poet to Jihadi: The Story of a Somali American in Minnesota" by Meira Svirsky. The Clarion Project, April 10, 2016. https://www.clarionproject.org/analysis/poet-jihai-story-somali-american-minnesota

Yet, at the age of 20, he began watching video sermons by Anwar al-Awlaki and "became enthralled with beheading videos."[215] By 2014, he had become the "emir" of a group of young men who had decided to go to Syria to join IS. He was arrested in 2015, and at his hearing he tried to explain what had changed him. "I was always listening to one side. I didn't see the other side of it, that innocent people were being killed." His duplicitous and self-serving explanation makes little sense given the rigid adherence to "Islamic purity" for which IS has become known, but adds some clarification to our understanding of the power of the IS message, how it indoctrinates, inspires, and draws in those already raised and educated to approve of jihad and shariah.

Is the U.S. in the IS Crosshairs?

On April 6, 2016, IS supporters released a video in which they called for new terror attacks in London, Berlin, and Rome. It was reminiscent of independent videos that appeared in the months after 9/11, which threatened new attacks on the U.S. by al-Qa'eda wannabes. This new video, produced in English by a group calling itself *al-Wa'ad* Media Production, presented the following message:

> *"If it was Paris yesterday, and today in Brussels, Allah knows where it will be tomorrow. Maybe it will be in London or Berlin or Rome. … Fight them, Allah will punish them by your hands … kill (infidels) wherever you find them."*[216]

More worrying than a vague threat from a group of IS supporters is the more imminent threat against U.S. troops stationed with the Multinational Force of Observers in the Sinai, where IS runs rampant and U.S. troops are forbidden to carry out offensive operations. And even more concerning than threats to our troops overseas are the ongoing threats by IS, directly against the U.S. homeland, and the knowledge that IS-inspired supporters are already known to be in all 50 states.

---

[215] Ibid.

[216] "ISIS supporters threaten UK with terror attacks in new propaganda video" by Lizze Deardon. *The Independent,* April 5, 2016. http://www.independent.co.uk/news/uk/home-news/ISIS-supporters-threaten-london-with-terror-attacks-in-new-propaganda-video-a6969006.html

The IS Threat to America – Is It Real?

At the time this book is written, America has been lucky. Although the FBI is investigating possible IS-connected threats in every one of the fifty states, there has yet been no major IS-directed or IS–inspired attack in the U.S.

But the threat does not always involve a direct, violent attack on civilians. On April 29, 2016, it was reported that IS hackers had posted a list of thousands of New York residents on-line, and urged IS followers to kill them. Although some of the information appeared to be outdated and law enforcement did not believe there was any credible threat, federal agents and NY City police made an attempt to contact all the people on the list, which included their names, home addresses, and email addresses.[217]

But even as IS appears to be concentrating its efforts on the capitals of Europe, its threats against the United States persist and should be taken seriously. The Islamic commitment that IS instills in its jihadis against the West includes America, which Islam's obligation to establish caliphate and shariah perceives as an obstacle that must be subjugated. Just days after the Paris attacks, IS released videos. In one they threatened to turn the White House "black with our fire, Allah willing" and in another, they used a recycled clip of a 'suicide bomber' with the threat to detonate his bomb in Times Square. In the first video, narrated in Arabic and translated by the Middle East Media Research Institute, the narrator says:

> *"We say to the states that take part in the crusader campaign that, by God, you will have a day God willing, like France's and by God, as we struck France in the center of its abode in Paris, then we swear that we will strike America at its center in Washington."*[218]

There are countless targets in every city and in every state across America that would serve the purposes of IS ideology to destroy the *kuffar* and our Constitutional system of individual liberty, equality for all before the law, and government by consent of the governed under rule of man-made law — all anathema to Islam. From the infrastructure that makes American industry

---

[217] "Islamic State-linked hackers post target list of New Yorkers" by Joseph Ax. Reuters, April 29, 2016. http://www.reuters.com/article/us-new-york-islamic-state-idUSKCN0XQ2AC

[218] 'The White House will turn black with our fire, Allah willing': ISIS warns of fresh attacks on Washington in the third video to threaten America in as many days" by Chris Pleasance. *Daily Mail*, November 19, 2016. http://www.dailymail.co.uk/news/article-3325952/The-White-House-turn-black-fire-Allah-willing-ISIS-warns-fresh-attacks-Washington-video-threaten-America-days.html

and commerce hum to the hubs of humanity that are the cities that have made America an icon in the world, from the centers of invention to the monuments that memorialize our heroes' contributions to the nation, all are targets for IS.

Targeting Civilians in Coordinated Attacks on Multiple Sites

An article on CNN.com reported, "Since declaring its caliphate in June 2014, the self-proclaimed Islamic State has conducted or inspired more than 70 terrorist attacks in 20 countries other than Iraq and Syria, where its carnage has taken a much deadlier toll; those attacks outside Iraq and Syria have killed at least 1,200 people and injured more than 1,700 others"[219].

The Islamic State's current jihad is hardly something new or unprecedented, of course. On December 26, 2008, one of the world's most grisly and horrifying jihadist attacks took place in Mumbai, India. The attack was planned and executed by an organization called Lashkar e-Taiba, in collaboration with ISI (the Pakistani intelligence service), al-Qa'eda, and members of the Indian underworld. The planning for this attack took over three years and required an enormous amount of organization. The series of coordinated attacks created a reign of terror that lasted for three days, in which a team of ten terrorists killed 164 people and injured more than 300. It became the 'gold standard' by which terrorists can measure their own operations, but few groups have the resources to carry out such a complex plan successfully. IS' considerable wealth makes it one of the few that does — and if or when backed by the resources of a nation state, as the Mumbai or 9/11 attacks were, the consequences obviously can be catastrophic.

The IS attack in Paris, on November 13, 2015, was modeled after the Mumbai attacks – a mini-Mumbai attack, with a team of terrorists simultaneously targeting multiple targets. It lasted only a few hours, but took almost as many lives. The team attacked six public places at roughly the same time, killed 130 people, and wounded at least 300 more. (The Mumbai attacks took 164 lives and wounded 304 more.) Although the Paris attacks were more limited than those in Mumbai, it may well be that IS has created a new standard that requires less planning, causes maximum damage, and commands optimum news coverage.

---

[219] "ISIS goes global: Over 70 attacks in 20 countries" by Ray Sanchez, Tim Lister, Mark Bixler, Sean O'Key, Michael Hogenmiller and Mohammed Tawfeeq, CNN.com, February 17, 2016. http://www.cnn.com/2015/12/17/world/mapping-ISIS-attacks-around-the-world/

America is full of soft targets, including shopping malls, cruise ships, theaters, restaurants, public transportation (except airplanes), sporting events, schools, and houses of worship, to mention only a few. For IS, all are appropriate targets for coordinated attacks as they carried out in Paris and Brussels, and all are potential elements of their master plan to turn America into an Islamic nation.

Individual Jihad Attacks

For many years, the FBI and Department of Homeland Security have been worried about and warning the American public about the potential for the so-called, misnamed 'lone wolf' terrorist attacks in the United States. In May 2015, Homeland Security Secretary Jeh Johnson warned, "We're very definitely in a new phase in the global terrorist threat, where the so-called lone wolf could strike at any moment."[220]

In government lingo, a 'lone wolf' is a single actor carrying out a terrorist attack on his or her own. In reality, there is no such thing as a 'lone wolf'. In every case, there is a "web of influence" behind the 'lone wolf'. What may look like a single person carrying out an action on his own is, in reality, the leading edge of a much larger set of influencing factors that have led to the 'lone wolf' attack. The connections may be strong, as in direct association with other jihadis, or they may be virtual, as with inspiration that comes via the Internet from websites or from communications on Facebook and Twitter. They may come through a mosque, through a friend, or through active membership in a terrorist cell. In the case of Islamic terrorism, that global network is called the *ummah* or worldwide community of Muslims, to which the individual jihadi owes an allegiance that always takes precedence over whatever citizenship may be indicated in identity documents or passports.

"It is important to recognize that individual jihad (or *fard 'ayn*) is an authoritative doctrinal concept within Islam. The obligation to defensive individual jihad is triggered whenever there is a *kuffar* military presence in any lands considered Muslim lands, because those lands are the homeland of all Muslims. The obligation to attack the *kuffar* wherever or however possible then transcends the obligation to one's family, parents, spouse or even slave

---

[220] "Lone-wolf terror attack could come at any time: Homeland Security secretary" by Aaron Short. *New York Post,* May 11, 2015. http://nypost.com/2015/05/11/lone-wolf-terror-attack-could-come-at-any-time-homeland-security-secretary/

master and does not require the order of a caliph to be binding on every Muslim, male or female, slave or free, in the world."[221]

One al-Qa'eda-linked case serves as a good example of the profound influence of the network behind the mistakenly-labeled "lone wolf" Nidal Malik Hasan. On November 5, 2009, the U.S. Army psychiatrist went to the Soldier Readiness Processing Center where he worked at Ft. Hood, TX, and fired over a hundred rounds into the soldiers gathered there. He took 14 lives, including one unborn child and one civilian, and wounded 30.

While the government was quick to call this an example of "violence in the workplace," the links connecting Hasan to a much wider network of jihad were clear, even before the attack. They included his mosque in Falls Church, Virginia, the notorious Dar al-Hijrah Mosque, and its imam, Anwar al-Awlaki. Al-Awlaki was an al-Qa'eda-linked Islamic preacher, who was a key influence behind many major terrorist attacks and plots against the West over a period of more than five years. Al-Awlaki later went to Yemen and became the voice behind AQAP's[222] *Inspire* Magazine. Hasan expressed admiration for the imam's teachings and exchanged a series of 18 emails with the imam, who became his inspiration and led him to jihad. Neither the Department of Defense nor the FBI, which investigated the Ft. Hood shooting, understood the significance of that email exchange; the deeply misleading Report of the DoD Independent Review, issued in January 2010, contained not one single use of the word "jihad."[223]

Two of the 9/11 hijackers, Nawaf al-Hazmi and Hani Hanjour, also attended the *Dar al-Hijra* mosque in Falls Church, VA, during the spring and summer of 2001. While it is not clear that Hasan knew or interacted with them, it is highly possible that they set an example for him eight years after 9/11. When the FBI reviewed his computer after the Fort Hood shooting, they found that he was a frequent visitor to jihadist websites, which also served as inspiration to him.

---

[221] Lopez, Clare, "Islam Commands Individual Jihad," *The Counterjihad Report*, December 18, 2011. https://counterjihadreport.com/2011/12/18/islam-commands-individual-jihad/

[222] Al-Qa'eda of the Arabian Peninsula, one of the most active franchises of al-Qa'eda

[223] "Protecting the Force: Lessons From Ft. Hood," Report of the DoD Independent Review, was issued in January 2010. http://www.defense.gov/Portals/1/Documents/pubs/DOD-ProtectingTheForce-Web_Security_HR_13Jan10.pdf Worse yet, three days after the Ft. Hood shooting, Army Chief of Staff Gen. George Casey appeared on ABC This Week and stated that he thought a "loss of diversity" would be an even greater tragedy than the massacre of his troops. https://www.youtube.com/watch?v=O8EITu5ZYo8

Part V 105

IS appears to prefer to send teams of jihadis to carry out foreign operations, perhaps lending more likelihood to the possibility of coordinated attacks in the U.S. as opposed to individual jihad suicide missions. Nevertheless, IS-inspired attacks remain a strong possibility wherever IS has motivated an individual to act alone, motivated by his or her network of influence.

High-Profile Individuals

On March 6, 2016, pro-IS hackers posted a "hit list" with the names and addresses of U.S. government officials on Twitter. Among the offices hacked were the Department of Defense, the Department of Commerce, the New Jersey Transit, and other law enforcement agencies. Accompanying this list was encouragement for carrying out "lone wolf" attacks on the individuals on the list.[224]

On March 7, the London Metropolitan Police warned that IS was seeking "spectacular attacks" on the West. The threat included police and military targets, but made reference to "something much broader."[225] Mark Rowley, national head of counter-terrorism, said that IS has been planning some "enormous and spectacular" terrorist atrocity on Britain and may have people trained to a paramilitary level to carry out attacks.

On March 8, an ominous IS video was released, warning the U.S., which they referred to as "protector of the cross," of upcoming attack similar to Paris. "We will kill, slaughter and burn your people very soon."[226]

The wider network supporting individual jihadis is ideal for IS operations in the U.S. In the summer of 2015, Reuters reported on an interview with FBI Director James Comey: "He said dozens of people in the United States who are suspected to be under the influence of Islamic State militants have 'gone dark' because of encrypted data."[227] When a jihadi network goes dark, it is an ominous sign, partly because they become much more difficult to track, and

[224] "ISIS Hackers Post U.S. Officials' Details Online, Urge Lone Wolf Attacks" by Anthony Cuthbertson. Newsweek, March 7, 2016.
[225] ISIS planning 'enormous and spectacular attacks', anti-terror chief warns" by Vikram Dodd. The Guardian, March 7, 2016. http://www.theguardian.com/uk-news/2016/mar/07/ISIS-planning-enormoU.S.-and-spectacular-attacks-uk-counter-terrorism-chief-warns
[226] "ISIS just issued direct threat to President Obama…[VIDEO]" by Michelle Jesse AllenBWest.com, March 9, 2016. http://www.allenbwest.com/2016/03/alert-ISIS-jU.S.t-released-video-with-new-threat-to-u-s-and-barack-obama/
[227] "FBI Says Arrests of ISIS 'Lone Wolves' Thwarted Deadly 4th of July Attacks" by John Hayward. Breitbart, July 10, 2015. http://www.breitbart.com/national-security/2015/07/10/fbi-says-arrests-of-ISIS-lone-wolves-thwarted-deadly-4th-of-july-attacks/

partly because it may be a signal that they are close to mounting an attack. Not being able to follow their activities puts law enforcement at a severe disadvantage as they try to stop what may be an imminent terrorist attack.

As early as July 2015, the U.S. government was deeply concerned about the advantage that deeply encrypted communications devices can give to jihadis to protect their secrecy. Reuters explained, "The Federal Bureau of Investigation is pushing technology companies to let law enforcement authorities have access to encrypted communications to investigate illegal activities. Those companies have resisted, arguing that such access would weaken systems against criminals and computer hackers." In the case of the FBI v Apple,[228] the point became moot when the FBI solved the decryption problem without the assistance of Apple.

Public Warnings and Public Threats

The coordinated attacks in Paris and Brussels, combined with the constant stream of threats on social media, had their effect. On March 22, 2016, the U.S. Department of State issued an unusual travel warning for Americans. It was for the whole of Europe and warned them of the *"potential risks of travel to and throughout Europe following several terrorist attacks, including the March 22 attacks in Brussels claimed by ISIL [sic]. Terrorist groups continue to plan near-term attacks throughout Europe, targeting sporting events, tourist sites, restaurants, and transportation."*

Immediately following the Brussels attacks, it became clear that although IS had not yet demonstrated that it had the ability to build bombs that could successfully be concealed in airport screening so it could be brought onto an airplane, it had clearly developed ways to make smaller bombs with larger impact than had been thought possible. In addition, the fact that one of the IS terrorists, Najim Laachraoui, was the bomb maker in the Paris attack, yet he blew himself up in the airport attack, suggests that IS has multiple bomb makers and that they are therefore expendable.

---

[228] In December 2015 the FBI acquired the iPhone of Sayeed Farouk, one of the two shooters in the San Bernardino massacre, but could not unlock the encryption password to access the data. They applied to the manufacturer, Apple, to unlock the phone, which the company refused to do, citing security concerns for its millions of customers. A lawsuit was filed, but later withdrawn when the FBI was able to use other resources to unlock the phone. The principle involved was a) whether the possibility of national security interests overrode the privacy of an individual, and b) whether the decryption of one phone might lead to reduced security and privacy of all users.

Forensic searches of the laptops, electronic intercepts, and documents revealed that other plots were also being planned, that several possible targets had been selected, and that these attacks were imminent. This is significant in light of the threats that IS continues to broadcast against Europe and the United States.

As the warnings from IS become more dramatic, more threatening, and more violent in their language, their intent seems to be growing stronger. At the end of March 2016, *al-Wafa* published a series of violent predictions that suggest that it intends to attack the U.S. in the heart of our nation, including Washington, D.C., and New York City.

In a translation published by the Middle East Media Research Institute (MEMRI), which monitors jihadi communications traffic, one IS article was published in late March 2016 with the title "America You Are Next." It began:

> *"America has forgotten that Muslims do not accept humiliation and will not forget to retaliate. ...*
>
> *"We haven't forgotten the screams of the virgin girls who were raped when you invaded Iraq. Today, with Allah's help, we will avenge them and restore every maiden's honor. Today we will blow up your honor, today we will eliminate your myth, today we will take your women captive and sell them at slave markets at prices reserved for the most unclean. Today we will take your children and raise them among Muslim children until they grow up, fight, and break the noses of those who remain among you."*[229]

With increasingly shrill and graphic threats coming from IS, the FBI and Department of Homeland Security are becoming increasingly alarmed. In an age when the pace of developing technology is rapidly accelerating, and the growing sophistication among jihadis is enabling them to pursue their goals more effectively, America needs to be smarter and better and faster in order to be able to anticipate and stop the attacks before they happen.

---

[229] As quoted in *The Washington Times* in "ISIS issues chilling warnings: More attacks targeting U.S., Europe are coming" by Rowen Scarborough. *The Washington Times*, March 29, 2016. http://www.washingtontimes.com/news/2016/mar/29/ISIS-social-media-warning-more-attacks-will-target/?page=all

CONCLUSION

On June 12, 2016, Americans woke up to a new terrorist nightmare. At 2 o'clock that morning, a heavily-armed man walked into Pulse, a large gay nightclub in Orlando, Florida, crowded with dancers and partiers. Twenty-nine-year-old Omar Mir Saddique Mateen was armed with a handgun and a rifle. Witnesses reported that he shouted "Allah hu akhbar" (Allah is greater) as he fired indiscriminately into the crowd. By the time the police finally stormed the building three hours later, 49 people had been murdered, 53 more were wounded, some critically, and the shooter was dead.

Two reports, coming just hours after the attack, linked Mateen to the Islamic State. According to Florida State Police spokesman David Procopio, witnesses reported that in the course of his three-hour rampage, Mateen himself made a 911 call in which he swore allegiance to IS and, specifically, to its leader, Abu Bakr al-Baghdadi. They also reported that he called the Tsarnaev brothers, perpetrators of the 2013 Boston Marathon massacre, his "homeboys."[230]

Shortly after the release of that information, the Islamic State itself took credit for the attack in a statement published by Amaq News, IS' official media outlet.

> **Amaq Agency**
> Source to Amaq: The attack that targeted a nightclub for homosexuals in Orlando, Florida and that left more than 100 dead and wounded was carried out by an Islamic State fighter.
>   👁 13   2:20 PM

This announcement gave credibility to its claim that Mateen was indeed connected in some way to the Islamic State. According to Aymenn Jawad Al-Tamimi (@ajaltamimi), Jihad-Intel Research Fellow at the Middle East Forum, "when a claim is posted via Amaq News it is a definitive IS claim,

---

230 "FBI: Orlando killer called Tsarnaev brothers his 'homeboys'" EagleTribune.com, June 13, 2016. http://www.eagletribune.com/news/fbi-orlando-killer-called-tsarnaev-brothers-his-homeboys/article_889930d0-3196-11e6-a966-77ca8a5dca7e.html

even though superficially it is not framed as such. ... People questioning 'source' framing of Amaq News don't get modus operandi as 'auxiliary outlet' of IS: it is an example of formal distancing."[231]

On the morning following the attack, Mateen's father, Mir Seddique, said that Omar had been angry after seeing two men kissing.[232] Because shariah law forbids homosexuality and IS executes gay men by dropping them off tall buildings or stoning them to death, Mateen's anger (and the event it may have triggered) was consistent with IS' application of shariah law and its particular hatred of gays. Mateem's depraved response was also consistent with the extreme brutality that characterizes the Islamist State.

It was the largest mass shooting in American history, and because it was also directly connected to the Islamic State, it was likely to be a seminal moment in America's long-overdue recognition of the real threat of jihad in the United States.

In his first statement to the nation after the massacre, the President called the attack "an act of terror," a dramatic departure from his usual reluctance to even mention the word terrorism when it is related, even remotely, to Islam. He indicated that this was being considered a Tier One event (the highest priority level), when he cancelled a high-level trip by senior officials to China as well as his own trip to Green Bay, Wisconsin, and he ordered U.S. flags to be flown at half-mast to honor the victims of the Orlando massacre.

Jihad on Our Doorstep

The trail of death that has become the hallmark of IS is no longer simply a local problem for the Syrians and Iraqis; it is a global problem that reaches across oceans, and threatens to get far worse in the very near future. IS has already exported its culture of torture and death to Paris, Cologne, Istanbul, Jakarta, Jerusalem, Bamako (Mali), Nigeria, Ouagadougou (Burkina Faso), the Philippines, San Bernardino, California, and Orlando, Florida. Whether IS-directed or indirectly-inspired by IS, these attacks continue to be a stunning reminder that the Islamic State is a force to be reckoned with and that it will not be crushed by anything less than an equally determined power greater than itself.

---

[231] Twitter.com @ajaltamimi June 12, 2016.

[232] "Omar Mateen got 'very angry' seeing two men kissing, father tells NBC"

On September 10, 2014, President Barack Obama made a formal statement[233] in which he said that [IS] "is not Islamic" but rather "a terrorist organization, pure and simple". He was wrong on both counts. IS is all about Islam, and everything IS does is connected to Islamic teachings as they are understood by its leadership. It is neither pure nor simple. Its structure, its operations, and its goals are deeply complex, and its motives are anything but pure. On the contrary, they are evil, depending on the suffering of others to achieve their goal for global domination. Yet, in his statement following the Orlando attack, the President refrained from linking the attack to Islam in any way.

Due to an unfathomable foreign policy, the United States missed the opportunity at the beginning of IS' power grab to stop its growth when it was not only possible but militarily feasible and relatively easy. The West now faces a far more dangerous and powerful terrorist organization whose complexity and life in the shadows make it infinitely more difficult to stop.

The IS battle plans come directly from the Koran. IS' savage rape of Iraq and Syria was based on Koranic teachings, a blueprint for what was yet to come. The Islamic State media warned the United States in clear terms that it was a target. The massacre in Orlando should have come as no surprise.

John Cantlie, a British prisoner of IS since 2012, expressed the threat succinctly in an article in the 14th issue of *Dabiq*:

> *"Make no mistake about it, the mujahidīn follow the Qur'ān to the letter, say what they mean, and mean what they say."[234]*

IS Attack in Brussels: A Case Study

The attack that took place in Brussels in March 2016 was an object lesson on IS and how it is operating beyond the Caliphate in Iraq and Syria. In the weeks that followed the Brussels attacks, more and more information began to come out regarding the details of how the attack was carried out and who was involved. Several stunning details about the attacks were revealed on April 10, a day after the capture of Mohamed Abrini. Abrini one of the leading participants in both the Paris and the Brussels attacks. In Brussels, he was the "man in the hat" before the airport attack.

---

[233] "Statement by the President on ISIL," Office of the Press Secretary, The White House, September 10, 2014. https://www.whitehouse.gov/the-press-office/2014/09/10/statement-president-isil-1

[234] "The Blood of Shame" by John Cantlie. Dabiq Issue #14, April 13, 2016, page 52.

The first stunning details to be released were that the network that planned and executed the two attacks was considerably larger than the authorities had originally thought and that its plans were considerably more extensive than expected. The massive store of weapons and explosives the terrorists had amassed for these attacks was found in their safe houses in the Brussels suburb of Schaerbeek, one placed just next door to a police station. When they were discovered after the Brussels attacks, they revealed just how ambitious and brazen their plans had been.

The second piece of information was that Brussels was not their original target. After the capture of Abrini, officials learned that it had been the intention of this IS jihadi group to attack Paris again in another horrific attack on La Defense, a section of Paris' business district where the headquarters of some of France's leading companies and multinational firms are situated and where many thousands of people work. Weapons and explosives were found, not only in their safe houses, but also in the same vehicle they had used during the Paris attacks.[235] But when the Belgian police began to close in on them, they abruptly changed their plans and carried out the attacks on the airport and the subway station in Belgium's capital.

The lessons learned from this new information was that IS has the ability to build large, strong cells composed of local jihadis who are prepared to attack in their own countries. It also revealed that they have the capacity for agile adjustment to the realities on the ground, to change their plans quickly and efficiently, to carry out the new plans effectively, and even to take advantage of a short window of opportunity effectively. It highlighted the links between IS and criminal networks, which helped the terrorists carry out their attacks. Finally, the linkage between the Brussels attacks and the Paris attacks which preceded them showed that IS has the ability to work across national boundaries in planning and deploying coordinated terrorist attacks.

In the issue of *Dabiq* #14, IS explained why the carnage in Paris and Brussels is central to their mission:

> *The death of a single Muslim, no matter his role in society, is more grave to the believer than the massacre of every kafir on earth ... the Shari'ah calls for the invasion of all kafir lands. ... This is an*

---

[235] "Brussels bombers planned new attack in France" April 11, 2016.
http://www.thedailychappaqua.com/2016/04/11/brussels-bombers-planned-new-attack-in-france-2/

obvious reality. Any disbeliever standing in the way of the Islamic
State will be killed, without pity or remorse, until Muslims suffer
no harm and governance is entirely for Allah.[236]

This is a warning not only for Europe, but for the United States as well. The
Islamic State is more than a rogue group of wild-eyed terrorists, slashing its
way across the Middle East and spreading mayhem wherever it goes. It is
more than an ideology-driven organization with an anti-West agenda. And it
is far more than a 'JV team' in the world of organized terrorism.

As a quasi-state with corporate discipline, global ambitions, and a terrorist
agenda, it wields a great amount of power in the areas it still controls. Not
unlike the Nazi war machine, IS puts great emphasis on organization,
record-keeping, and strict top-down authority. Its growth and the amount of
territory that it was able to acquire in a few short years is unprecedented in
world history. But in light of its subsequent loss of territory in the face of a
concerted effort by coalition and Iraqi forces, IS has, true to form, reinvented
itself into an international terrorist organization, recruiting from and
operating on foreign soil.

IS' Plan for Growth

On May 23, 2016, the *International Business Times* (IBT) reported[237] that IS was
planning a "violent Ramadan" during the Islamic holy month, which would
begin on June 6. Not unlike those of other religious groups, Muslim holy
days are times for prayer and reflection. But for Muslims imbued with the
spirit of jihad, these days are also an appropriate time for action against the
infidel, because jihadis believe their martyrdom will be greater if they die
during the holy month of Ramadan.

On June 9, 2016, IBT reported the release of a video by one of IS' media arms,
al-Furqan Media, in which IS spokesman Abu Mohammed al-Adnani "called
on supporters to carry out more attacks on the West during the Islamic holy
month of Ramadan 'to win the great award of martyrdom.' "

Then, in early June, the "United Cyber Caliphate," a pro-IS group, released a
31-minute video in which it revealed what it called a "kill list" with the

---

[236] "Foreword," *Dabiq* Issue #14, April 13, 2016, page 4.
https://azelin.files.wordpress.com/2016/04/the-islamic-state-22dacc84biq-magazine-1422.pdf
[237] "Isis encourages more attacks during Ramadan in latest audio message" by Lara Rebello.
International Business News, May 23, 2016. http://www.ibtimes.co.uk/isis-encourages-more-attacks-during-ramadan-latest-video-message-1561426

names of more than 8,000 people, most of them Americans and more than 600 of whom live in Florida. Their "kill list," thought to be the longest ever produced by IS, was a virtual directory of the names, addresses, and emails of thousands of people from around the world.[238]

Of the roughly 8,000 names, 7,848 were found to belong to U.S. residents: 1,445 in California, 643 in Florida, 341 in Washington, D.C., 333 in Texas, 333 in Illinois, and 290 in New York. Another 312 names belonged to people living in Canada, 69 names belong to Australians, and 39 names and addresses belong to people living in the UK. "The remaining names on the list targeted individuals living in Ireland, France, Italy, Belgium, Sweden, Germany, Estonia, Greece, Brazil, Guatamala, New Zealand, South Korea, Jamaica, Trinidad and Tobago, and Israel." The UCC released the list in a post in both Arabic and English on the encrypted messaging app Telegram. Supporters were urged to "follow" those mentioned in the list and "kill them strongly to take revenge for Muslims."[239]

IS' Shrinking Land Holdings Equals a Growing Global Threat against the West

The loss of some 45% of its territory and economic resources made IS even more reckless beyond the borders of its Caliphate. As significant parts of the land it captured in Iraq and Syria were lost, IS doubled down on its attention to the war against the West, and its presence abroad metastasized. The IS mission not only continues, it grows in a different and even more menacing direction. Even as it suffers a dramatic loss of territory, it is redirecting its efforts to the international arena, coopting existing networks in Europe and the U.S., and using them to forward its campaign of jihad against the West. The Islamic State is still strong and resilient, and its menace against its perceived enemies is more intense than ever.

In an effort to further spread its influence abroad, IS leadership took a leaf from the al Qaeda strategic playbook, and began decentralizing some of its activities abroad. Where it was formerly a rigid top-down organization, it now encourages individual jihadis to carry out missions on their own,

238 "Longest-ever Isis 'kill list' including over 8,000 people released by United Cyber Caliphate" by India Ashok. International Business Times, June 9, 2016. http://www.ibtimes.co.uk/isis-longest-ever-kill-list-targeting-over-8000-people-released-by-united-cyber-caliphate-1564450

239 Isis encourages more attacks during Ramadan in latest audio message" by Lara Rebello. Intenational Business Times, May 24, 2016. http://www.ibtimes.co.uk/isis-encourages-more-attacks-during-ramadan-latest-video-message-1561426

sometimes providing training and logistical support. The Islamic State has reinvented its top-down micro-management of its war to allow and even encourage so-called "lone wolf" jihadis to act on their own. It encourages its supporters to carry out their jihad in their own communities, where they know their environment and where they can move around in relative freedom.

The flood of immigrants, infiltrated with IS fighters who have been pouring into the countries of Europe, has already destabilized entire societies and put an unbearable economic burden on countries that can ill afford it. What appeared at first to be a humanitarian decision to allow the immigration of hundreds of thousands of Middle Eastern 'refugees' into Europe (more than 1.26 million in 2015, according to the EU statistics agency[240]) has turned into a human nightmare of lawlessness and relentless demands for economic benefits that exceed the countries' economic capabilities.

The radicalization that has taken place in the schools and mosques in Europe has also created immense problems for the Europeans. IS' networks throughout the continent are deep and complex, and the same process is now being exploited in the United States as well.

What has already happened in Europe should have been a warning to the U.S. government of what we could expect here. But the Obama administration, rather than learning from Europe's recent history, has accelerated the immigration of thousands of Middle Eastern 'refugees' into the heartland of America.

IS has made it clear that it is sending its soldiers to infiltrate this mass migration and enter America's cities in this unprecedented flow of humanity. The FBI confirms that many are already here. Porous borders, an accelerated program of immigrant resettlement, and an administration hell-bent on bringing as many Muslims into the country as possible (regardless of how limited its vetting process is), all point to a growing disaster waiting to happen in the United States. America's current immigration policy is a spark in search of a gas leak.

In June 2016, IS celebrated the second anniversary of the establishment of its Caliphate, coinciding with the start of the holy month of Ramadan.

---

[240] "EU refugee crisis: asylum seeker numbers double to 1.2m in 2015" by Jennifer Rankin. The Guardian, March 4, 2016. https://www.theguardian.com/world/2016/mar/04/eu-refugee-crisis-number-of-asylum-seekers-doubled-to-12-million-in-2015

According to a Reuters report, IS released an audio early that month, urging its supporters to carry out their attacks during "Ramadan, the month of conquest and jihad. Get prepared, be ready … to make it a month of calamity everywhere for the non-believers … especially for the fighters and supporters of the Caliphate in Europe and America."[241]

Make no mistake, the Islamic State is at war with the West. It recruits fighters from global sources, encouraging local supporters to carry on the war against the "infidels" on their own home turf. With such a newly decentralized "army" of jihadis, hidden among the Muslim communities around the world, the Islamic State is an even more formidable force to be reckoned with than it ever was.

IS has proven that it has both the will and the agility to change its strategy rapidly and forcefully. No sooner did the mass Syrian migration to Europe begin than IS mobilized to send thousands of its own fighters into the flow of humanity to give itself a secret, solid presence in Europe. They were able to mobilize quickly. The Paris and Belgium attacks were a demonstration of the effectiveness of this strategy.

The growing number of individual attacks on local residents and the dramatic rise of sexual assaults on women and children throughout Europe are further indications of how effectively IS is infiltrating Western countries and disrupting their national cultures. The fear which now pervades many areas of Europe and the chaos that this is creating is symptomatic of IS' larger plan to spread its brand of Islam into the West. The Orlando attack demonstrated organization and planning, and has reawakened the fears that were first felt on 9/11 and have once again been sown in the U.S.

Simply put, IS has become an unprecedented threat, not only as a terrorist organization fighting its jihad, but also as an existential threat to Western society as we know it. It has already demonstrated that it can grow exponentially and strike anywhere in the world at a time and place of its choosing. The traumatic changes that have already taken place in Europe's way of life should raise red flags for all Western countries, particularly the United States, which is a prime target for IS.

---

[241] Ramadan Violence: Islamic State Urges Lone Wolf Attacks in U.S., Europe" by Edwin Mora. Breitbart.com, May 24, 2016. http://www.breitbart.com/national-security/2016/05/24/ramadan-violence-islamic-state-urges-lone-wolf-attacks-in-u-s-europe/

Although IS is not the only threat facing the United States today, but it is one America cannot afford to take lightly. The massacre in Orlando is likely to be only the beginning of a new and violent campaign by the Islamic State against the United States. Our ability to confront these threats depends upon America's willingness to take them seriously, to call the enemy by name, and to address the threat aggressively and decisively. This is a war America cannot afford to lose. And the time to mobilize against it is now.

America: PC Nation and Victim of Islamic Terror or World Leader?

Whatever happens next, in America and abroad, it is not likely to be business as usual. America's policy of ignoring the warnings of a boastful IS and making access to the heartland easy for the advance guard of IS fighters will open the gates to a new and dangerous American landscape. The lives of Americans will change dramatically as the threat from IS terror becomes a day-to-day reality, not unlike what Israelis have been living with for years.

The worst mistake that America can make is to continue to demand a politically correct society, making endless allowances for the misuse of American freedoms to advance an Islamic agenda, and living in the fantasy that "it can't happen here." It is already happening in Europe, changing the bedrock culture of centuries. Given the government plan for importing tens of thousands of "Syrian refugees" without the ability to screen them, and the continuing flow of unscreened illegal immigrants over our southern and northern borders, it was only a matter of time before IS visited our door here in the United States.

The atrocities that occurred in Orlando were a stark reminder that a complacent America will once again have to suddenly face "the morning after" when, without warning, another deadly terrorist attack on the homeland changes everything. Orlando was another wake-up call that Islamic jihadis will stop at nothing to achieve their goal for an Islamic world.

Only a strong and determined America, whose leadership is willing to stand up to the tyranny of political correctness and the barbarous conduct of the Islamic State, will be able to destroy the IS threat and keep America safe and free.

# # #

APPENDIX I

BIOGRAPHY OF IS FOUNDER ABU MUSAB AL-ALZARQAWI
AND THE BIRTH OF THE ISLAMIC STATE

Abu Musab al-Zarqawi's odyssey began with his first visit to Afghanistan in 1989, as a young, low-level foot soldier. Born Ahmad Fadeel al-Nazal al-Khalayleh on 20 October 1966 in the small Jordanian mining town of Zarqa, he was known as a petty criminal and street thug before heading off to join the *mujahedeen*. He arrived there just as the war was winding down, but managed to fight in a few engagements and work as a journalist before returning to Jordan. According to Mary Anne Weaver's biography of al-Zarqawi,[242] written for Atlantic Magazine, his decision to fight for Islam began not long before departing for Afghanistan when he met up with missionaries from Tablighi Jama'at[243] from whom he learned about orthodox Muslim practice and "returned to Islam."

In Afghanistan, al-Zarqawi met another personal connection who would prove especially important in his future: Abu Muhammad al-Maqdisi, the Palestinian-born Salafist cleric whose teaching about an Islamic government's obligation to rule according to shariah would be so influential for both al-Zarqawi and the Global Jihad Movement. Both al-Maqdisi and al-Zarqawi returned to Jordan in 1993, where their immediate involvement in a series of botched terrorist operations landed them in jail by 1994.[244] Al-Zarqawi was sentenced to fifteen years in prison, but only served six before being released from prison in December 1999 thanks to a general amnesty declared by Jordanian King Abdullah II. The time that al-Zarqawi spent in prison along with al-Maqdisi was deeply transformative. Reportedly, while in jail, al-Zarqawi wrote several tracts, which were posted on the Internet, and came to the attention of Osama bin Laden.

---

[242] "The Short, Violent Life of Abu Musab al-Zarqawi" by Mary Ann Weaver. *The Atlantic,* July/August 2006. http://www.theatlantic.com/magazine/archive/2006/07/the-short-violent-life-of-abu-mU.S.ab-al-al-Zarqawi/304983/

[243] Gateway to Jihad: Tablighi Jama'at" by Ilana Freedman.

[244] Stern, Jessica and J. M. Berger, "ISIS: The State of Terror," March 12, 2015. https://bi.hcpdts.com/reflowable/scrollableiframe/9780062395566

Immediately after getting out of jail, al-Zarqawi headed back to Pakistan. In December 1999, he crossed over into Afghanistan, where he met Osama bin Laden for the first time. [245] Although bin Laden found al-Zarqawi brash and disrespectful, he saw something in him that led to giving al-Zarqawi permission to set up a training camp in Herat in western Afghanistan. It was the young man's first official leadership role. He called his camp Jund al-Sham, or Soldiers of the Levant, and gave himself the title "Emir of Sham."[246]

Over the following years, al-Zarqawi was funded by bin Laden with Mullah Omar's approval, traveled throughout the region, recruited new fighters, and grew his network. Despite never having acceded to bin Laden's request that he pledge *bayat*, after 9/11, when the U.S. forces invaded, al-Zarqawi fought for bin Laden and the Taliban, was injured, and eventually fled to Iran in late 2001.[247] There, the Iranian regime, which had been deeply involved together with al-Qa'eda in the 9/11 attacks,[248] provided him medical care, then saw him off in later 2002 to the Khurmal and Sulaymaniyah areas of Iraqi Kurdistan, where he set up a chemical weapons lab, which allegedly produced ricin and cyanide.[249] That area of Iraqi Kurdistan formerly had been under the control of the Kurdish Sunni jihadi leader, Mullah Krekar, who led the Ansar al-Islam opposition group since the 1990s against Saddam Hussein's regime. Al-Qa'eda scouts had made an arrangement with Krekar, however, more than a full year before September 2001 that he would relinquish his group and its territory when asked. This he did, moving to live permanently with his wife and children in Norway after 9/11 (where they'd earlier obtained refugee status).

Whatever al-Zarqawi's relationship may have been with Saddam Hussein's regime, and however counterintuitive it may seem for one who spewed Sunni hatred for the Shi'a, his closest backers from the time he arrived in Iraq forward were the Iranian forces of the Islamic Revolutionary Guard Corps

---

[245] "The Short, Violent Life of Abu Musab al-Zarqawi" by Mary Ann Weaver. *The Atlantic*, July/August 2006.

[246] Ibid.

[247] Stern and Berger

[248] See the Havlish case at http://iran911case.com/, in which Judge George Daniels, Southern District of New York, ruled in December 2011 that Iran and Hizballah were co-responsible for the 9/11 attacks. See especially Exhibit #6, http://information.iran911case.com/Exhibit_6.pdf, by Clare M. Lopez and Dr. Bruce Tefft, which details the history of the Iran/Al-Qa'eda relationship.

[249] MSNBC report, March 2, 2004

(IRGC), who provided arms, explosives, medical care and safehaven whenever needed by his fighters.

Once in Iraq, al-Zarqawi began to make a name for himself almost immediately by orchestrating a series of dramatic terrorist attacks. On August 7, 2003 a car-bomb attack at the walled Jordanian embassy[250] in Baghdad killed at least eleven people and wounded over a hundred. Twelve days later, a bombing at the United Nations headquarters[251] killed twenty-two people, including top United Nations envoy in Iraq Sergio Vieira de Mello, and dozens more were wounded.

Then, on August 29, 2003, al-Zarqawi orchestrated the a car bomb attack that killed more than a hundred people outside Shia Islam's holy shrine in Najaf.[252] The Imam Ali shrine is one of Shi'a Islam's holiest sites, housing the grave of the man who founded the Shi'a sect. The bomb had been hidden in the trunk of a car, near one of the entrances to the shrine, and was set to go off immediately after the Friday midday prayers, when Ayatollah Mohammed Baqr al-Hakim would leave the shrine. The charismatic "Sayid,"[253] one of the most prominent and beloved Shi'a clerics in Iraq, had been groomed by Iran to become Iraq's first Shi'a leader, before he was killed in the attack. At least 100 other people also died in that bombing, and over 500 were wounded. With these three well-calculated attacks, al-Zarqawi plunged himself and Iraq into a nightmare of savage sectarian violence that would make him the symbol of resistance to the American-led Coalition presence in Iraq.

In May 2004, al-Zarqawi ordered a notorious wave of hostage beheadings, which he videotaped, in addition to a never-ending series of suicide and truck bombings of Shi'ite shrines and mosques. He also orchestrated the assassination of U.S. diplomat Laurence Foley, a senior administrator at the U.S. Agency for International Development (USAID), who was murdered in front of his home in Amman, Jordan. The Iranian regime fully supported

---

[250] "Car Bomb Attack at Jordanian Embassy in Baghdad" by Associated Press. AugU.S.t 7, 2003. Fox News. http://www.foxnews.com/story/2003/08/07/car-bomb-attack-at-jordanian-embassy-in-baghdad.html

[251] "Top UN envoy Sergio Vieira de Mello killed in terrorist blast in Baghdad" AugU.S.t 19, 2003. UN News Service. http://www.un.org/apps/news/story.asp?NewsID=8023#.VlDUJtC4l0s

[252] "Twelve years on, remembering the bomb that started the Middle East's sectarian war" by Bobby Ghosh. AugU.S.t 28, 2015, Quartz. http://qz.com/476191/remembering-the-bomb-that-started-the-middle-easts-sectarian-war/

[253] "Sayid" is an Arabic language honorific denoting a claim to direct descent from the bloodline of Muhammad.

attacks by and against terror militias both Sunni (al-Qa'eda/Abu Musab al-Zarqawi) and Shi'ite (Badr Corps, Jaish al-Mahdi) and the vicious civil war they deliberately provoked, because Tehran calculated this strategy would best support its ultimate objective: to oust the American and Western presence from Iraq and replace it with its own. In the long run, the strategy has worked exactly as planned.

In October 2004, after months of difficult negotiations, al-Zarqawi pledged *bayat* (allegiance) to Osama bin Laden and the two men entered into a mutually beneficial relationship. It gave al-Zarqawi added prestige to be a part of al-Qa'eda, and gave bin Laden a dedicated presence in Iraq, which he badly wanted. Al-Zarqawi's organization became Al-Qa'eda in Iraq (AQI). On December 27, 2004, Al Jazeera broadcast an audiotape of bin Laden, in which he referred to al-Zarqawi as the "Emir of Al Qaeda in the Country of Two Rivers" (the Tigris and the Euphrates).[254]

Thirteen months later, on November 10, 2005, al-Zarqawi is believed to have been behind the targeting of three upscale Amman hotels by suicide bombers, killing 57 and wounding at least 110.[255]

Finally, on June 7, 2006, al-Zarqawi was killed in a targeted assassination in which a USAF F-16 dropped two 500-pound bombs on the safe house in which he was staying.[256]

---

[254] Iraq Ablaze: Inside the Insurgency by Chehab, Zaki 2006, IB Tauris & Co, Cornwall, p. 8.

[255] "3 Hotels Bombed in Jordan; At Least 57 Die," by Hassan M. Fattah and Michael Slackmannov. *The New York Times,* November 10, 2005.
http://www.nytimes.com/2005/11/10/world/middleeast/3-hotels-bombed-in-jordan-at-least-57-die.html

[256] "At Site of Attack on Al-Zarqawi, All That's Left Are Questions". By Dexter Filkins and John F. Burns, John F. *The New York Times.* June 11. 2006.

APPENDIX II

ISLAMIC STATE
BUHUTH AND 'IFTAA COMMITTEE
FROM THE RELIGION'S MAXIMS ON CAPTIVITY AND ENSLAVEMENT

Prepared by the Buhuth and 'Iftaa Committee

TEXT (in Translation)

In the name of God, the Compassionate, the Merciful

Praise be to God the Lord of the Worlds, and prayers and peace be upon our Prophet Muhammad, and all his family and companions. As for what follows:

Indeed it is well-known that God the Exalted has not mandated anything except for great wisdom and exalted purpose, so the Exalted has not ordered anything unless there is also in it the great good, and there is no prohibition on anything except there is also in it harm that God is aware of.

Therefore, the one who looks at the secrets of the shariah, and the one who ponders on the elevated divine maxims, let him stand in awe before the greatness of God Almighty's wisdom in His power, and the greatness of God Almighty's blessing in His law.

The let him be even more certain in his witnessing the perfection of this shariah and what has emerged from wisdom, mercy, honour, power and perfection. Thus is the shariah of the Wise, the Merciful, the Great, the Powerful- for the qualities of God are exalted in His law.

And among the matters that have been legislated in the shariah is the captivity of the women of the disbelievers at war and their enslavement.

For the disbelievers who have no pact of the dhimmi, ceasefire or security between them and the Muslims, the principle regarding them is that their blood and property are free for pillage if they do not convert to Islam or pay the jizya and enter under the rule of shariah.

In this regard their women and offspring may be taken captive and it is not allowed to murder the women in principle if they provided no assistance in the war against the Muslims. And this Shari'i ruling is established in the Book [Qur'an], the Sunna and Ijmaa' [scholarly consensus].

And this requires the stipulation of a number of points, including:

1. It is not allowed to take captives of the Muslim woman or enslave the Muslim man from first principles, since the reason for enslavement is disbelief.

2. It is not allowed to take captives of the women of the disbelievers not waging war from the people of the Dhimma [i.e. Jews and Christians] and the like.

3. The captivity of the women of the disbelievers waging war and their enslavement must be through jihad in that they are sabaya (female prisoners of war).

4. It is not allowed to take the sabaya as slaves before the ruling of the Imam [i.e. the Caliph] upon them because he may rule to be benevolent towards them or ransom for them. Therefore it is not allowed to lie carnally with them or enjoy them simply for being sabi (captive), but also the Imam must make divisions among them [and thus] if they are allowed to be taken as slave girls, the possessions of one's right hand, then one can lie carnally with them according to Shari'i conditions.

5. The Imam may be benevolent towards them by letting them go and not enslaving them etc.

From maxims of the captivity and enslavement of the women of the disbelievers waging war

Indeed the objectives and benefits that are realized in the captivity and enslavement of the women of the disbelievers waging war are numerous and great, dazzling the human mind that is incapable of finding solution to the problems of human societies. For captivity and enslavement are a guarantor to solve many of the problems and impediments, in addition to its great fruits and benefits that include:

1. Captivity and enslavement are a means of spreading Tawheed [Islamic monotheism]

Indeed Tawheed is the greatest objective for whose sake we have been created, and it is the objective of the sending of the Messengers and the revelation of the Books, just as jihad in principle has been mandated for the sake of Tawheed as God Almighty said: "And fight them until there is no more fitna and religion belongs entirely to God"- Sura al-Anfal 39 [Qur'an 8:39].

Similarly Tawheed is the principle of man's happiness and thus the extent of his true, everlasting life, for if man loses Tawheed, he loses everything. If he attains success in Tawheed, he attains success in eternal blessing and happiness.

Therefore Tawheed has been the greatest blessing by which God has blessed His servants.

So when the Muslims make captives of the women of the disbelievers at war and enslave them, we have therefore brought these women out from their environment tainted with shirk [idolatry] to a new authentic environment far removed from all the influences of shirk and decadence- as what that encompasses from life for them is totally different from what came before- and a psychological breakdown that is inevitable. And with what they see from the glory of Islam, they will eventually have recourse to Islam voluntarily or out of obligation. And thus one of them becomes closer to Islam than disbelief, and so it will be gradually, until they enter into Islam.

And with the passing of days and months, Islam becomes firmly established in the heart, so their Islam is sound. And this is something the Ummah has witnessed through history.

Thus captivity and enslavement becomes for these women among the greatest blessings of God upon them, as on account of it they escape eternity in the Hellfire. [Emphasis by Editor's]

For on the authority of Abu Huraira (may God be pleased with him): from the Prophet (SAWS): he said: "God wondered at people entering Paradise in chains" (narrated by Bukhari).

And on the authority of Abu Umamah: he said: "The Messenger of God (SAWS) laughed, so we said: 'What makes you laugh oh Messenger of God?' He said: 'I wondered at people being led in chains to Paradise'" (narrated by Ahmad).

Ibn al-Jawzi said: "Its meaning is that they were taken prisoner and put in bonds but when they got to know the truth of Islam they entered into it voluntarily so they entered Paradise, so the compulsion to imprisonment and bondage was the first cause" (Fath al-Bari 6/145).

And Bukhari produced in his authentic collection on the authority of Abu Huraira (may God be pleased with him) regarding the Almighty's words: "You were the best Ummah brought out for the people"- he said: "The best people for the people, bringing them in chains on their necks, until they should enter into Islam."

2. In captivity and enslavement is a demonstration of the honour of Islam and its people.

There is no doubt that the captivity and enslavement of the women of the disbelievers at war and their offspring are among the greatest forms of the honour of Islam and its shariah, as it is a clear affirmation showing the supremacy of the people of shariah, and the greatness of their affairs, and the dominance of their state, and the power of their might.

If offensive jihad is limited to killing the disbelievers at war and the apostates and fighting them, as well as inflicting harm and damage to them, and plundering what we can from their property and wealth, then jihad of realization gathers with all that captivity and enslavement of the women of the disbelievers at war and dividing them up among the mujahideen, and sanctioning their genitals [i.e. carnal relations with them]. And that is the sign of realization and dominance by the sword. And it has been said:

"And the girl of spouse whom our arrows have given in marriage [i.e,. for sex], it is permissible to consummate the marriage with her [i.e., lie carnally with her] even if she has not been divorced."

And all this is in accordance with God Almighty's words: "And to God, His Messenger, and the believers belong honour, but the hypocrites don't know it" (Sura al-Munafiqun: 8) [Qur'an 63:8].

3. In captivity and enslavement is the lowering of disbelief and its people.

Imam Ahmad brought out in his chain of transmission from Ibn Omar (may God be pleased with him) from the Prophet (SAWS): he said: "I was sent before the Hour with the sword, until God alone should be worshipped with no partner for Him, and my livelihood has been placed under the shade of my spear, and lowering and humiliation have been placed for whosoever violates my order, and whosoever imitates a people is of them."

For God has struck the disbelievers who have violated the command of God and the command of His Messenger (SAWS) with lowering and humiliation, and among the sins of this humiliation imposed on them is the captivity and enslavement of their women and the permissibility of their genitals.

And this is an objective in angering and psychologically vanquishing the disbelievers when they see their honour as captives among the people of Islam, and it is of disgrace for them. So Ibn Abi Hatem narrated in his transmission from Qatada regarding the Almighty's words about the Jews: "For them is disgrace in this world." He said: "This means: what God brought on the Qurayza people from captivity and killing, and the Nadhir people from their expulsion."

And likewise captivity and enslavement for the disbelievers have been a source of sorrow and exasperation for them, as well as a penalty for their disbelief in God because the penalty is from the type of deed, for when they have deviated from God the Exalted's religion, have been haughty about Tawheed of God and have refused to worship God alone, God has allowed for us to take them captive and enslave them, for they have become slaves and servants among the monotheist servants of God: God Almighty has said: "And the one whom God humiliates, there is no one to ennoble him" (al-Hajj 18) [Qur'an 22:18].

4. Captivity and enslavement are of the Sunnah of the Prophet.

Indeed making captives of and enslaving the women of the disbelievers at war are a revival of prophetic Sunnah, for the Prophet (SAWS) used to enslave the women and offspring of the disbelievers at war and that occurs in many well-known incidents, including:

The Prophet (SAWS) took the women and offspring of the Banu al-Mustaliq captive, just as Bukhari narrated in his authentic collection: that the Prophet

(SAWS) launched a raid on the Banu al-Mustaliq while they were off-guard and their cattle were drawing water. So he killed the fighting men and took their offspring captive...

And similarly the Prophet (SAWS) took the offspring and women of the Banu Qurayza as captives when the Banu Qurayza annulled their pact, and he killed their men while seizing their wealth.

Likewise the Prophet (SAWS) took captives from Hawazin [an Arab tribe] in the Hanin raid until the captives reached 6000 maidens in number....[1]

And also the Ahl al-Seer mentioned that the Prophet (SAWS) had four slave girls (concubines) [2], and they were: Maria, and she was the mother of his son Ibrahim, Rayhana, a girl he acquired among some of the captives, and Jariya given to him as a gift by Zaynab bint Jahash.

And Bukhari headed a section in his authentic collection: Section of Taking Concubines.

5. Captivity and enslavement are a mercy from God for the women and offspring of the disbelievers.

Indeed God's mercy is applicable for all created, even the disbeliever, for indeed God's mercy encompasses him in this world, for he is given sustenance, food, dwelling and settlement, and all this is from God's mercy on him. God Almighty has said: "Our Lord, You have encompassed everything with Your mercy and knowledge" (Ghafir 7) [Qur'an 40:7].

Therefore making captive of the women and offspring is a mercy from God for them, because this captivity and enslavement are the practical and realistic means to save these women from waste and desolation, and it is the most useful way of protecting them from atrocities and find protectors for them and their offspring.

For whenever the disbelievers refuse to enter into Islam or give the jizya or enter under the rule of shariah, there remains no other option at that point except for us to attack them, fight them, kill them, take prisoners from them, lie in wait for them, surround them and catch them...so they become either killed, taken prisoner or driven out.

So the problem stands out of the women and offspring of those who did not aid them in the war against the Muslims, for it is not allowed to murder them in principle and this is from God's mercy on them, but despite what happened to their disbelieving society from expulsion, fragmentation and collapse, we find that these women are now without a career, provider or breadwinner.

And thus they have entered into a new societal framework. If all human minds were to come together for solutions relevant to this new situation to be found, they would be utterly incapable.

Therefore we find that the most useful means to protect these women from waste, desolation and poverty, and the way to guarantee a stable life for them: making captives of them and enslaving them.

Because the master and possessor of one of them is entrusted by law to raise her prestige, spend money on her and provide her with food, drink and residence, while keeping her from the forbidden practices. But also with the need of the one made captive and enslaved for social relations and sexual intercourse, we find that there has come in the shariah allowance to enjoy sabaya (slave girls) and lie carnally with them.

So therefore this person made captive and enslaved should be provided with residence, security, stability, food and drink. And thus she should be able to escape from atrocities and vices, and living in the ways and canals of garbage.

And this is from the mercy of this shariah as well as its justice, glory and wisdom.

6. Showing the mercy of shariah and its justice in dealing with slave girls and slaves.

Captivity and slavery have been present throughout history, even such that some of the Arab tribes used to bury their daughters alive fearing captivity and poverty. And the sources of enslavement among the disbelieving nations were numerous, not limited to one path.

And the dealing of the disbelieving nations with slave girls and slaves was only for the sake of oppression, humiliation contempt for them. And the slave girls and slaves were entrusted with tasks that that they could not tolerate or manage, so their life amounted to one of bodily torture and being psychologically vanquished.

As for the shariah of Islam, the situation is completely different, for it has come ordering for mercy and gentleness towards them, and justice with them, being good to them.

For God the Exalted has ordered us to be good towards slaves and slave girls. God Almighty has said: "And worship God and do not associate any partners with Him. And be good to parents, relatives, orphans, the wayfarers, the near neighbour, the far neighbour, the companion beside you, and those whom your right hands possess. Indeed, God dislikes those who are self-delusional and arrogant" (Nisa' 36) [Qur'an 4:36].

And there has come encouragement to educate them, call them to Islam, and discipline them. For Bukhari narrated on the authority of Abu Mousa (may God be pleased with him): he said: the Messenger of God (SAWS) said: "Whoever has a girl and teaches her, is good to her, and then emancipates and marries her, he has double the remuneration."

Also there has come the prohibition on calling them (my slave and slave girl) as Bukhari on the authority of the Prophet (SAWS): that he said: "Not one of you should say: 'Feed your lord, place a light for your lord, but rather he should say: 'Sayyidi, Mawlaya.' And not one of you should say, 'My slave, my slave girl.' But he should say: 'My boy, my girl, my servant.'

And Bukhari translated this hadith by these words of his: "Section on dislike of insolence towards the companion."

And the shariah has stipulated the principle of brothers in religion between the free and enslaved Muslims. For the Prophet of Mercy (SAWS) said as Bukhari narrated in his authentic collection: "The slaves are your brothers, so feed them from what you eat."

And SAWS said: "Indeed your brothers are your chattel, whom God has placed under your hands, so whoever has his brother under his hand, let him feed him from what he eats, and dress him with what he wears, and do not entrust them with what overcomes them, so if you entrust them with what overcomes them, assist them."

Observe the sublime gentleness as Bukhari narrated in his authentic collection on the authority of the Prophet (SAWS): he said: "When the servant of one of you brings his food, and if he does not sit with you, then let him eat at least a morsel or two or a dish or two, for he is the guarantor of his treatment."

And so we find that the Prophet (SAWS) forbade hitting the slave's face as disciplinary action, just as Bukhari narrated in his authentic collection. He said: "Section: if he hits the slave, let him avoid his face." And he drew out a hadith of the Prophet (SAWS): "If one of you fights, let him avoid the face."

And likewise there has come encouragement to emancipate the believing necks as per God Almighty's words: "Loosening a neck [*i.e.*, freeing a slave], or feeding on a day of severe hunger, a closely related orphan" (al-Balad 13-15) [Qur'an 90:13-15].

And the Prophet (SAWS) said: "Whichever man emancipates a Muslim man, God has saved him in every part of him from the Hellfire" (narrated by Bukhari).

7. In captivity and enslavement is generosity on men who are incapable of marrying.

And this is from God's mercy on men who cannot find marriage or for whom the matter of marriage is difficult from expenditures and the like, so God has allowed them to have concubines in the possession of the right hand (slave girls). God Almighty has said: "And those who guard their genitals except from their wives or what their right hands possess, for they are not blamed" (al-Mu'minun 5-6) [Qur'an 23:5-6].

And this generosity is something by which the mujahideen benefit most, and perhaps this is of the kind of reward for the type of work, for the mujahideen are the ones who have excelled in their times with their spouses to God- Almighty and Exalted is He- until one of them whose separation from his spouse lasts for a long time because of *ribat* [frontline duty] and expeditions, or he may be a muhajir who has left a spouse and children behind him, so there is long-lasting exile upon them, and the exile upon them intensifies, so this divine grace and wondrous generosity brings captivity and enslavement.

Likewise it is from generosity upon men to be allowed to take women captive and purchase them, and this is something by which unmarried men benefit most or the one who desires multiple [spouses] but cannot be just, so for him is the possession of the right hand as wealth.

God Almighty has said: "If you fear that you cannot deal justly with the orphan girls, then marry whosoever pleases you from the women: two, three or four. But if you fear that you cannot be just, then only one or what your right hands possess. That is more suitable, lest you be inclined to be unjust" (Nisa' 3) [Qur'an 4:3].

8. Captivity and enslavement are a means of increasing the offspring of the Muslims.

There is no doubt that increasing numbers is strength for the Muslims, and the fact that the concubine slave girls may give birth is not an ugly or condemnable matter. For Ibrahim- peace be upon him-took Hajer (may God be pleased with her) as a concubine and from her was born Ismail, peace be upon him.

And the Prophet of God Suleiman (peace be upon him) had many concubines.

And as mentioned before the Prophet (SAWS) took Maria (may God be pleased with her) as a concubine and she was the mother of his son Ibrahim.

And Ali ibn Abi Talib (may God be pleased with him) took a concubine from the captives of the Bani Hanifa, and she bore for him Muhammad who became known as Ibn al-Nafia, and likewise a number of the Companions (may God be pleased with them) took concubines.

And throughout history there have stood out great men from the leaders of the Muslims who were sons of concubines (slave girls) like Sayf al-Din Qutuz who led the battle of Ayn Jalut against the Tatars [Mongols]. And similarly al-Nasir Muhammad bin Qalawun at whose hand many of the Crusaders' fortresses collapsed.

Conclusion

This is an exposition on some of the maxims on captivity and enslavement, and we do not claim its confinement and restriction to what we have mentioned, for God has ruled on many of His rulings, giving us an insight into His blessing and grace on some of them, while He conceals others: "Above every possessor of knowledge is One who knows more" (Yusuf 76) [Qur'an 12:76].

And indeed it is from the blessings of God Almighty on the Muslims in this age in which the tribulations and afflictions have been many that He has established for them the Islamic State, which has revived the glories of the Ummah, and has strived to renew what has been wiped out from the path.

For it has arisen as the statement of Tawheed, the best statement, and it has waged war on shirk and its people by the pen and the sword, and it has established judiciaries and muftis, and has opened institutions and schools, and has imposed the jizya on the people of the Book [Jews and Christians], and has enslaved the women and offspring of the disbelievers.

[...]

Al-Buhuth & Al-'Iftaa Committee

[Notes from the original text]

[1] - See: al-Tabaqat al-Kubra by Ibn Sa'ad (2/116), 'Alam al-Nabwa by Al-Mawardi (6/268), al-Muntadhim fi Tarikh al-Umam wa al-Muluk by Ibn al-Jawzi (3/239) and Zada al-Mu'ad by Ibn Qayyim al-Jawzia (3/415).

[2] - Sabaya cannot be made slave girls simply as sabi (prisoner) but when the Imam imposes slavery upon them and distributes them among the mujahideen thus they become slave girls as those possessed by the right hand, and thus they are called al-Jarari, and if this Ummah takes them up for sexual intercourse, so they are also called: "Surayya"... and its plural: "Sarari." The Hafidh Ibn Hajar said: "I called it thus because it is derived from tasarrur and its origin is from al-sirr and it is among the nouns of sexual intercourse, and also there is said for it istisrar, or it may also be that it is called thus in the main part the issue of her is concealed from the wife" (Fath al-Bari: 9/126).

APPENDIX III

ISLAMIC STATE (IS) RELEASES PAMPHLET
ON FEMALE SLAVES

December 4, 2014

The Research and Fatwa Department of the Islamic State (IS) has released a pamphlet on the topic of female captives and slaves. The pamphlet, dated Muharram 1436 (October/November 2014) and printed by IS's publishing house, Al-Himma Library, is titled *Su'al wa-Jawab fi al-Sabi wa-Riqab* ("Questions and Answers on Taking Captives and Slaves"). It was apparently released in response to the uproar caused by the many reports this summer that IS had taken Yazidi girls and women as sex slaves.

Written in the form of questions and answers, it clarifies the position of Islamic Law on various relevant issues and states, among other things, that it is permissible to have sexual intercourse with non-Muslim slaves, including young girls, and that it is also permitted to beat them and trade in them.

The Islamic canon relies here especially on the Sunna, because Muhammad is reported to have approved of and engaged personally in slavery, rape of captured girls and women, and sex slavery. Because of the Qur'an's depiction in numerous places (Q 33:21 for one example) of Muhammad as the *Insan al-Kamil* (or perfect man), subsequent consensus of the scholars (*ijma*) fixed such practices firmly within permitted activity for all Muslims for all time.

The following report is a complementary offering from MEMRI's Jihad and Terrorism Threat Monitor (JTTM).[257]

Below are excerpts from the pamphlet, which was posted on a pro-IS Twitter account.[258]

Question 1: What is al-sabi?
Al-Sabi is a woman from among *ahl al-harb* [the people of war] who has been captured by Muslims.

Question 2: What makes al-sabi permissible?
What makes *al-sabi* permissible [*i.e.*, what makes it permissible to take such a woman captive] is [her] unbelief. Unbelieving [women] who were captured and brought into the abode of Islam are permissible to us after the imam distributes them [among us].

Question 3: Can all unbelieving women be taken captive?
There is no dispute among the scholars that it is permissible to capture unbelieving women [who are characterized by] original unbelief [*kufr asli*], such as the *kitabiyat* [women from among the People of the Book, *i.e.*, Jews and Christians] and polytheists. However, [the scholars] are disputed over [the issue of] capturing apostate women. The consensus leans towards forbidding it, though some people of knowledge think it permissible. We [IS] lean towards accepting the consensus...

Question 4: Is it permissible to have intercourse with a female captive?
It is permissible to have sexual intercourse with the female captive. Allah the almighty said: '[Successful are the believers] who guard their chastity, except from their wives or (the captives and slaves) that their right hands possess, for then they are free from blame [Qur'an 23:5-6]'...

Question 5: Is it permissible to have intercourse with a female captive immediately after taking possession [of her]?
If she is a virgin, he [her master] can have intercourse with her immediately

257 For JTTM subscription information, visit http://www.memrijttm.org/subscription.html
258 Twitter.com/U112842, December 3, 2014.

after taking possession of her. However, if she isn't, her uterus must be purified [first]...

Question 6: Is it permissible to sell a female captive?
It is permissible to buy, sell, or give as a gift female captives and slaves, for they are merely property, which can be disposed of [as long as that doesn't cause [the Muslim ummah] any harm or damage.

Question 7: Is it permissible to separate a mother from her children through [the act of] buying and selling?
It is not permissible to separate a mother from her prepubescent children through buying, selling or giving away [a captive or slave]. [But] it is permissible to separate them if the children are grown and mature.

Question 8: If two or more [men] buy a female captive together, does she then become [sexually] permissible to each of them?
It is forbidden to have intercourse with a female captive if [the master] does not own her exclusively. One who owns [a captive] in partnership [with others] may not have sexual intercourse with her until the other [owners] sell or give him [their share].

Question 9: If the female captive was impregnated by her owner, can he then sell her?
He can't sell her if she becomes the mother of a child...

Question 10: If a man dies, what is the law regarding the female captive he owned?
Female captives are distributed as part of his estate, just as all [other parts] of his estate [are distributed]. However, they may only provide services, not intercourse, if a father or [one of the] sons has already had intercourse with them, or if several [people] inherit them in partnership.

Question 11: May a man have intercourse with the female slave of his wife?
A man may not have intercourse with the female slave of his wife, because [the slave] is owned by someone else.

Question 12: May a man kiss the female slave of another, with the owner's permission?
A man may not kiss the female slave of another, for kissing [involves] pleasure, and pleasure is prohibited unless [the man] owns [the slave] exclusively.

Question 13: Is it permissible to have intercourse with a female slave who has not reached puberty?
It is permissible to have intercourse with the female slave who hasn't reached puberty if she is fit for intercourse; however if she is not fit for intercourse, then it is enough to enjoy her without intercourse.

Question 14: What private parts of the female slave's body must be concealed during prayer?
Her private body parts [that must be concealed] during prayer are the same as those [that must be concealed] outside [prayer], and they [include] everything besides the head, neck, hands and feet.

Question 15: May a female slave meet foreign men without wearing a hijab?
A female slave is allowed to expose her head, neck, hands, and feet in front of foreign men if *fitna* [enticement] can be avoided. However, if fitna is present, or of there is fear that it will occur, then it [i.e. exposing these body parts becomes] forbidden.

Question 16: Can two sisters be taken together while taking slaves?
It is permissible to have two sisters, a female slave and her aunt [her father's sister], or a female slave and her aunt [from her mother's side]. But they cannot be together during intercourse, [and] whoever has intercourse with one of them cannot have intercourse with the other, due to the general [consensus] over the prohibition of this.

Question 17: What is al-'azl?
Al-'azl is refraining from ejaculating on a woman's pudendum [*i.e.,* coitus interruptus].

Question 18: May a man use the al-'azl [technique] with his female slave?
A man is allowed [to use] *al-'azl* during intercourse with his female slave with or without her consent.

Question 19: Is it permissible to beat a female slave?
It is permissible to beat the female slave as a [form of] *darb ta'deeb* [disciplinary beating], [but] it is forbidden to [use] *darb al-takseer* [literally, breaking beating], [*darb*] *al-tashaffi* [beating for the purpose of achieving gratification], or [*darb*] al-*ta'dheeb* [torture beating]. Further, it is forbidden to hit the face.

Question 20: What is the ruling regarding a female slave who runs away from her master?
A male or female slave's running away [from their master] is among the gravest of sins...

Question 21: What is the earthly punishment of a female slave who runs away from her master?
She [i.e., the female slave who runs away from her master] has no punishment according to the shariah of Allah; however, she is [to be] reprimanded [in such a way that] deters others like her from escaping.

Question 22: Is it permissible to marry a Muslim [slave] or a kitabiyya [i.e. Jewish or Christian] female slave?
It is impermissible for a free [man] to marry Muslim or kitabiyat female slaves, except for those [men] who feared to [commit] a sin, that is, the sin of fornication...

Question 24: If a man marries a female slave who is owned by someone else, who is allowed to have intercourse with her?
A master is prohibited from having intercourse with his female slave who is married to someone else; instead, the master receives her service, [while] the husband [gets to] enjoy her [sexually].

Question 25: Are the huddoud [Qur'anic punishments] applied to female slaves?
If a female slave committed what necessitated the enforcement of a hadd [on her], a hadd [is then] enforced on her – however, the hadd is reduced by half within the hudud that accepts reduction by half ...

Question 27: What is the reward for freeing a slave girl?
Allah the exalted said [in the Qur'an]: "And what can make you know what is [breaking through] the difficult pass [hell]? It is the freeing of a slave." And [the prophet Muhammad] said: "Whoever frees a believer Allah frees every organ of his body from hellfire."

About the Author

ILANA FREEDMAN is a veteran intelligence analyst specializing in Islamic terrorism and its impact on the Middle East and the West. Trained in Israel, where she lived for sixteen years, she has been an advisor to law enforcement and industry in counter-terrorism.

Freedman is author of several hundred articles published in the national and local press and on her blogs at GerardDirect.com and FreedmanReport.com.

INDEX